# "Do I Know You?"

## "Do I Know You?"

# "Do I Know You?"

## Living Through the End of a Parent's Life

---◆---

## BETTE ANN MOSKOWITZ

## Kodansha International

*New York • Tokyo • London*

Kodansha America, Inc.
114 Fifth Avenue, New York, New York 10011, U.S.A.

Kodansha International Ltd.
17-14 Otowa 1-chome, Bunkyo-ku, Tokyo 112, Japan

Published in 1998 by Kodansha America, Inc.

Library of Congress Cataloging-in-Publication Data
Moskowitz, Bette Ann.
"Do I know you?" : living through the end of a parent's life /
Bette Ann Moskowitz.
p.   cm.
Includes bibliographical references.
1. Aging parents—United States—Family relationships.
2. Aging parents—United States—Psychology.   3. Aging parents—
Care—United States.   4. Adult children—United States—Family
relationships.   5. Mothers and daughters—United States.   I. Title.
HQ1063.6.M665   1998
306.874—dc21   97-38240
ISBN 1-56836-210-2

Book design by Bernard Klein

Manufactured in the United States of America on acid-free paper

98 99 00   10 9 8 7 6 5 4 3 2 1

*For My Sister*

# Contents

# Acknowledgments

MY thanks to the New York Foundation for the Arts, whose fellowship for the early pages of this project provided the concrete encouragement that helped me complete it.

Thanks, for sharing knowledge, stories, and expertise to: Thelma Abrams, Violet Crump, Gereese Gambino, Jeanette Gray, Pnina Kass, Meri and Herb Kaufman, Sylvia Moss, Gideon Panter, M.D., Christine Pennington, Marion Renning, Helen Stern-Richter, Samona Sheppard, Judy and Marty Silverstein, Judith Summerfield, Brenda Tanfield, Dolores Vlismas, Bette Weidman, Doris Wizbicki, and Carol Wojciechowski.

Thanks again to Judith Summerfield for her insightful and critical first reading, and to Sandra Taub, Ph.D., and Esther Feingold, for early encouragement.

Thanks to Jonathan Dolger for his steady advocacy.

Thanks to my children, Lynnellen and Michael, and

to my children-in-law, Joe and Lori, for their loving concern for their grandmother, and their support of me.

Thanks to Al Levine and Marvin Moskowitz for their time and tenderness in helping my sister and me care for our mother and to Marvin Moskowitz for his love, friendship, and for helping me keep my head on straight for the last thirty-five years.

My wonderful sister, Norma Levine, in the writing of this book, was invaluable: confirming and correcting facts, dates, stories; she was a patient and critical listener, an unflagging believer that the job could be done, and an emotional support at the lowest of times. We became partners in order to take care of our mother, and in so doing, reclaimed our sisterhood and became dear, close friends. To her go my biggest thanks of all.

# *Preface*

I began these notes a long time ago, as a way of settling the pain and bringing some order to the confusion I felt when my mother began to decline in health and memory. I wanted to try to understand what she was going through, and to examine what life is like in the extreme circumstances of old age, which, from what I see, include isolation, debility, loss of memory, respect, and bladder control. After a while, I began another set of notes, of practical information, things I learned while looking for the answers to crucial questions about housing, medical care, financial, legal, and other help for my mother (or me in aid of my mother). In time, I wanted to explore the possibility of "life" in such a place as a nursing home, and what an increasingly long-lived society is supposed to do with all those extra years. This book is a combination of all of those notes. It isn't precisely a how-to-find book or a what-to-think book, and I have largely ignored the economics of geriatric care because this has been written about in other places and by other people. Though I have talked to experts, the authority I assert comes from having gone through the process of helping, and finally, taking over the decision about where my mother would spend her last days. This is the book I would have wanted to *be* there when I was going through it: something that would have given me, at various times, what I needed in the way of helpful suggestions, testimony, reassurance, and support.

It is a rumination on what it means to put a parent "away" and what it is like to live with that reality. I mean it to be useful and reflective, but not conclusive. As of this writing, my mother is still alive, and as those "last days" turn into years, I am still unsure whether the decisions my sister and I ultimately made for her were the right ones. My thoughts change daily.

This is also my mother's story. And since she is its heroine and all that I know is filtered through the scrim of her experience in old age, this book is not meant to be objective, or scientific. Sometimes it will be about me and my family, as well as my mother, in her last home. In this confessional age, where intimacies are the common currency, I have no particular desire to up the ante. Yet, what I have seen and experienced may be of help to other children of aging parents, and I offer it in this spirit.

———

MY mother was born Mamie Tolbin, one year and twenty days into the twentieth century: January 20, 1901, in New York City. For the next ninety-two years she lived in just a few places: with her parents in upper Manhattan, with her husband and two daughters in the Bronx, with her husband again (after my sister and I had married and moved on) in Long Beach, New York. After my father closed his business and she retired from teaching, they became snowbirds and went to Miami Beach for the winter months, coming back to Long Beach in the spring and staying all summer.

When my father died, at seventy-five, my mother, almost immediately, moved to Miami Beach permanently, to a small studio apartment overlooking the ocean on Collins Avenue. It was the first home she had ever had that was hers alone, not as someone's daughter, not as someone's wife. She left behind all the fine, staid, well-made furniture of her young and middle-aged life, and started out fresh, refurnishing with bright golds, unexpected greens, hopeful yellows, very unlike anything we would have imagined she would choose. She loved that apartment. She kept it spotlessly clean. You weren't allowed to open the heavy off-white draperies because the sun would fade the gold sofa, but you could sweep them aside as many times as you wished to enjoy the incomparable view of the ocean and the horizon, which she was as proud of as if she had created it herself.

In her building was a whole community of mostly retired elderly people. They had a library, recreation rooms, a sundeck. The residents played cards, took classes, and had parties. In this community, it mattered less whether you were rich or beautiful than whether you were well-preserved. Health and strength equalled royalty. And so my mother was a queen, respected, even adored. And she took to it and thrived, seeming positively *released* into this widowhood and old age, uncorseted at last, with the time and inclination to finally have fun. Formerly reticent, she became something of a party animal. She went to dances and did the cha-cha. She played cards and mah-jongg and joined the committee that planned social events and edited the house newsletter. She started yoga lessons at eighty-four and watercolor lessons at eighty-five. She went to retired teachers' association luncheons and met old colleagues and students. She had time to read as much as she liked. (It had always been her one gluttony and now she indulged it, going to the public library—the one in her building was too limited—at least once a week, and "using up" a steady supply of paperback novels I sent her faster than I could replenish them.)

She had made the move to Miami without consulting my sister or me; unafraid of being alone, and unconcerned about getting old, she built herself a grand new life.

Her only concessions to old age were the scraps of paper we got used to seeing lying around the apartment —near the phone, in a dresser drawer, even on the sink drainboard—with our names and addresses and phone numbers and the words "If anything happens to me, notify . . ." And one day she told us, unsentimentally, that she had arranged to have her body shipped to New York when she died, to save us the fuss and expense.

My sister and I both knew that it was her wish to live to the end of her life in this, her (in a sense) first home. Once, seeing a particularly frail and deranged old person in the street, my mother said in her characteristically blunt way, "If I ever get that bad, take me out and shoot me."

In 1988, when she was eighty-seven, I could not imagine her ever getting that bad, or becoming unable to take care of herself. I had no plans for it if she did. (Though I could certainly have imagined a quick "shooting" more easily than any of the more normal alternatives, such as a nursing home, home care, or living with one of us.) I knew very little, in fact, about the process of aging. I imagined senescence as a uniform ebbing of the tide of mind and knowledge, slipping back to sea, so to speak. I learned in the ensuing months and years that it is more like acid hitting a tea towel: big holes appeared randomly, and yet there were inexplicable strong spots where the fabric held. It was possible to see the intact parts only and not the holes. It was possible to fold and re-fold the tea towel for a long time, and that is what I and my sister did.

The signs that my mother was declining mentally and physically were, at first, small and occasional. They progressed slowly, and sometimes seemed to disappear. This caused confusion and contradictions and indecisions in how to view what was happening. We often did not know what was cause for alarm and what was a temporary condition. We did not know whom to ask. We sometimes didn't know what to ask. Is *this* behavior normal? Is *that*? Who tells you a thing like that? A doctor? A nurse? People who want to sell you their service or brand of care? Whom do you trust? What are the signs that a person cannot any longer take care of herself? What is minor? What is major? When is the right time to intervene in a person's life, and take a custodial role? Doesn't it depend on the person? And aren't we the ones who know our person better than anyone else?

But we didn't.

If this period of time was a depressing and upsetting one for my sister and me, it was most certainly terrifying for my mother. How busy she must have been hiding her disabilities behind her back, managing to circumvent her lapses and distract us (and herself) from noticing them when they occurred, at the same time conserving her energies and watching cracks in the sidewalk so she wouldn't trip when she walked.

Did she remember to take her blood pressure pills? How do you know these things long distance? Do you disbelieve what she tells you? How do you make changes, big and small, when someone is unwilling to change? How do you talk to someone about her own decline? Our difficulties were surely compounded by my mother's fiercely independent character and our generally obedient daughterly sensibilities. She could still raise her voice, scold us sharply, and we would back down. "Of *course* I remember to take my pills!" Conversation closed.

We talked with people, kept our eyes and ears open, read the occasional article, but no case seemed to be quite like our mother's, and no one else's solution seemed to satisfy. We disagreed with one another quite often, each one interpreting the things we saw and heard in different ways. My sister was generally more observant of my mother's decline—I felt *too* observant —and she made too much of little things. She felt I didn't see enough, or that I minimized things I should have paid more attention to. I was opposed to any kind of institutional living for my mother, whether an adult care facility or a nursing home, knowing she'd rather be shot than live in such a place (and feeling the same way myself). Her apartment was too small for a live-in companion, if she would have considered such a thing, which she would not.

The one thing my sister and I agreed on was that my mother could not live with either of us, something my mother would have, up until the very last, considered *her* last option as well.

For a long time, I thought that if we could drag it out long enough, my mother would simply close her eyes, and that would be that. But the reality was not so simple. She proved too strong to die and not strong enough to survive intact, and so in the end she had to leave her beloved apartment and nobody took her out and shot her. On an autumn day in 1992, she entered a nursing home in Long Beach, New York, and she is there now, as I write this. But it wasn't the end, it was another beginning.

"How is old age?" I ask her. She has several answers. One of them is "It stinks." But another day, she shrugs and says, "Same as everything else. But you move a little slower and you don't eat as much."

So my mother remains: honest, practical, with a survivor's sense of humor. This is her story.

*"Do I Know You?"*

# PART ONE

———◇———

# The Decline

*"Don't send anyone to help me.
If they come, I won't let them in."*

## Miami Beach, March 1988, Age Eighty-seven

SHE falls.

She says she has tripped on the edge of a rug and twisted her ankle. She calls for a taxi and takes herself to the emergency room of the hospital, where she is treated for a bad sprain. She takes herself home. We only learn about this after the fact when she calls my sister to let us know what happened.

"Can you believe it?" we ask each other. "What a woman!"

Other people say "God bless her!"

She herself says it's nothing to make a fuss about.

Yet this is what we hear other people talk about; and what we have feared might happen. *You go along fine and then all of a sudden they fall. And you're not there to help.*

Despite her successful handling of the situation, we think of it as a narrow escape. She refuses to wear an "I've-fallen-and-I-can't-get-up" alarm, and she doesn't want to talk about moving back to New York where she can be close to us in an emergency.

"I can take care of myself," she says. But we are unnerved.

## Miami Beach, June 1988

SHE is coming to Long Beach, New York, for the summer, as she usually does, and because of the ankle injury, she needs help in packing and traveling.

I fly down. (My sister and I have begun to split the tasks, roughly according to our schedules and temperaments. She does daily check-ins, and I do the flying rescue.) I arrive in the early afternoon as scheduled, right on time, but she is relieved that I haven't crash landed. Typical of her to worry. Being terrified for her children's safety is her way of loving us. I hated it when I was young but now that I'm older, it seems kind of nice that there is still someone on this earth that worries irrationally about me as I now worry about my kids.

After I drop my bags, she wants to take me to see the ocean. So we leave the packing for later and go across the street to the ocean.

Her ankle is almost healed. She is on a walker, but just for security, she says. She says she is not taking it with her up north. It makes her look crippled. She holds up her leg for a second, flexing it, like a showgirl. The ankle is slightly swollen but I note the firm, shapely calf, an athlete's leg. She was an early women's tennis champion and is still proud. She also believes that sickness or injury is a matter of personal weakness, an embarrassment. Nonetheless, I say, she should take the walker for security. We argue about it. She handles the walker (and me) with authority, stopping traffic on Collins Avenue to cross.

The recent art deco restoration of South Beach has not reached my mother's section of Collins Avenue, the main street that runs all the way up to Fort Lauderdale. Here, on this stretch of Collins, it's still seltzer not salsa. The deco colors on the hotel facades are the originals, from the thirties and forties, faded as old ribbons, powdery blues and grays; the neon signs, occasionally with a letter blown, are yesterday's elegant names of exorbitant Shangri-las, now charming only because of how outdated they are: the Delmonico, the Edec Roc, the Cadillac, or my favorite, the Malabo (which always sounds to me like Malibu with a Jewish accent). Here, the old of Miami Beach—brisk or bedraggled, skin like leather, cane-toting, walker encircled, little-sweater-over-the-shoulder in ninety degree heat, dazed or functioning, down-and-out or well-preserved—still own the street.

My mother is feeling good. She has just had her before-going-up-north checkup and her doctor says she is in great shape. Her blood pressure is down. Last week she had a momentary weakness that seemed to settle in her arm and deaden it, but it went away. The doctor wanted her to go for some kind of test, but she didn't. Why should she, as long as it went away? She tells me this as she tells everything, definitely, decidedly. It occurs to me that I have never spoken to my mother's doctor. It occurs to me that other children of elderly parents think nothing of calling up their parents' doctors and checking up on them. Why do I feel that it would be disrespectful to call him without her knowledge? (*With* her knowledge is out of the question.)

When we get back to her apartment, I see her clothes are strewn all over the place, in and out of the suitcases. She sits in a chair and I hold up each item; she says "take it" or "leave it" and I pack it or lay it aside. She has thirty pairs of shoes. Some of them are twenty years old, leather cracked, soles scraped thin. She hasn't worn some of them in years. We laugh about this shoe mania, which I have inherited. I try to talk her into throwing some of the shoes away, but she won't part with even one. "Not now," she says. We have a hard time eliminating the ones she won't take to Long Beach. There has always been a quality of eccentricity in my mother, a sort of counterbalance to her devotion to propriety, little hints of excess, which, in a playful mood, she is willing to admit. The shoes are one of its emblems. (Another is the extent of her devotion to propriety itself, I think. Or the way she extends the idea of propriety to include hiding her feelings; shows of emotion are seen as weakness. Never much of a kisser or hugger, she stiffens her body against incoming embraces.) Today, when I joke about the shoes, she seems not to get it. I have a sudden sense I am "handling" her.

I put the clothes we are leaving behind back in the dresser. This is the first time I have seen the inside of her dresser drawers. They are in a terrible tangle. I wonder, is this at odds with my mother's reputation for neatness? Or isn't it? I try to remember if the outward neatness always hid an inner disorganization. Was this the way she was when I was growing up? I think so. I remember looking for something in a messy top drawer. Then I think not. I tell myself I think so, but I really don't know if I have composed it out of my storytelling mind or not; if it is something new, is it a bad sign?

Her refrigerator is empty. There is absolutely nothing there. "What have you been eating?"

"There's plenty to eat," she says. "There's crackers, there's some cream cheese."

There are six stale crackers in a Premium box, and a crumpled cream cheese wrapper with nothing inside. There is not even milk. "How do you drink your coffee?" I ask.

"I'll drink it black," she says. She gave everything away to her neighbors; she has to clean out before she leaves for the summer. But her cupboards are bare, too. There are few provisions, no tuna fish, no evaporated milk, no jelly jars, no peanut butter. None of the usual things she stocks. It is as if she has been "spending down" her food, so that *it* would end just at the same time as she did. Is this consistent with her personality or is it a sign of depression? What has she been eating? While she was telling us she was all right, getting around all right with the bad ankle, was she really suffering? Starving? Is it my imagination, or does she look thin? Has that pan on the stove always had a burnt bottom?

She says she will take me out to dinner, but it is clear that was not the plan: She can't walk easily, I don't have a car, she is exhausted, and our flight is early the next morning. So I go shopping and come back with the equivalent of a dinner: some prepared salads, tuna fish, cheese, a French bread, a bottle of white wine. She is frantic. I bought enough for an army. Who is going to eat all that? What is she going to do with everything? I make a mistake. I say we can throw away what we don't eat. She becomes terribly upset and stays upset all the way through the meal, and when she sees me pour left-over wine down the drain, she goes wild. I know my mother is testy, but this agitation seems to have another color, and another speed.

At the airport, I order a wheelchair for when we get to Kennedy. My mother does not like our assigned seats on the plane, and, though it is a full flight, the attendant kindly switches us to an aisle seat near the exit. But there is a noisy child two seats away and my mother begins complaining loudly and insisting on another seat change. Fuming, I tell her to stop. I try to explain that there is nowhere for us to go, but she is adamant. Fortunately, the mother and child move. When I have described my mother, I have always said her bitchiness was like a brine; it pickled her and kept her young. Now, I ask myself, "Is this not a woman who still has command and control of her life and can influence the world around her?" But with the asking comes the implication that I have begun to have my doubts.

## Long Beach, New York, Summer 1988

WE have the opportunity to see my mother almost every day. Our confusion intensifies, and so do our conflicts. In some ways, she seems as vigorous in mind as ever. It is the summer my first novel has been published. When I hand her the book, she, the great reader, sits down right then and there, with everyone around her, and begins to read. She enjoys the fact that I have acknowledged her in the credits, but she raises her eyebrows at me calling her a "great fighting woman." I know it is the "fighting" she objects to; it is not quite her idea of a compliment.

She sees a lot of her grandchildren this summer. They

visit and hang out with her, enjoying her still snappy, slightly outrageous takes on the people and the world around her. She has a practical, sometimes brutal, honesty which they get a kick out of. My son, who has a summer job driving around making deliveries for a local business, stops off to see her often. Sometimes he takes her shopping, or for pizza, one of her food loves. He talks to her about his future and respects her advice, even though it always includes "finish college" which he is not sure he wants to do. "You know grandma and school," he says. He opposes strongly any notion that she is failing at all. He gets angry when we bring it up and defends her, seeing the *thought* as some sort of sneak attack. She is still reading a lot. My friend Paula and I supply her with stacks of paperbacks and there is always an open book on her bed. She even keeps her hand in at teaching: the seven-year-old next door climbs over the terrace to visit and play with her and she discreetly tests his vocabulary. A traveling salesman who lives on her floor comes for coffee and sympathy. She was right about the walker; she gets along fine without it.

Yet, she is definitely repetitive and forgetful. And she is not eating much. She gets furious with me when I bring groceries or food that I have baked or cooked. One day she says to me, "When are you going to bring me some of your stuffed cabbage?" and when I bring it to her, she asks my sister why I am bringing her this stuff, she doesn't want it. My sister does better: She brings prepared food, and my mother permits this, though often she does not eat it. Instead of feeling a comfort in having plenty of food, as my sister points out, she gets almost hysterical when there is too much in her refrigerator, as she had that last day in Miami when I bought dinner. She has always been finicky, I remind my sister. She never sat at the dinner table, but ate standing up, stealing tastes, in between serving my father and sister and me, as if hunger were just another weakness. Now she seems to have lost interest even in her old treats, like ice cream and Almond Joys. I wonder if too many choices have begun to confuse her, but when I ask her, she tells me she isn't as active anymore as she once was so she just isn't as hungry. This sounds logical to me and I am quick to accept it. My sister is not, and when she suggests my mother may be forgetting to eat, I get angry and, like my son, defend her against this "assault."

She still enjoys shopping and window shopping, though. This summer we take her to Alexander's, and Filene's Basement, and the five-and-ten, which is her favorite. Each time we go to the five-and-ten she buys socks and sponges. When my sister takes her and her friend Lilly to the supermarket ("I start each one— ladies, start your engines, on your mark—at a different aisle," she says), my mother glides up and down the aisles happily, stocking up on paper goods. She has duplicates of paper napkins, paper towels, toilet paper. Added to what I brought, she could stock a public toilet for a week, and when I look under the sink, I see enough sponges to make a small rug.

She gets (typically) testy when Lilly asks my sister to make another stop on the way home. She doesn't like sharing her daughters with anyone, and she likes doling out our favors carefully. She doesn't want anyone treating us like schmucks.

One day she tells my sister that she was sleeping with her finger up in the air, and someone came in and took the ring off it. And, indeed, her wedding band is gone. We search everywhere for it. We even wonder about the traveling salesman who comes to visit her, but he was on the road at the time of the ring's disappearance. We question her closely. My sister points out to her that her story is absolutely impossible, but she will not change it. My sister is concerned and I am generally dismissive. So she gets a crazy idea in her head now and then. What's the harm? And so what if she doubles up on paper goods? It all seems benign enough to me. Still, we fantasize for a moment about how great it would be if we could somehow get Julia—the live-in maid who was with our family for fifteen years—to come and stay with her in Florida. But Julia is now a sick and aging widow herself and anyway it is impossible, she and my mother would never get along. Both of us stop short of imagining we have to take my mother in or that she cannot go back to Florida to live by herself.

At this time we notice she is buying sanitary pads, to control occasional bladder incontinence. I suggest (and even buy for her) one of the more appropriate and comfortable diaperlike products, but she denies she has a problem.

In the middle of the summer, she suddenly refuses to play in the almost-daily canasta games she used to love. Lilly and the other "girls" can't coax her to play. She won't even go out to lunch with them. She seems to withdraw from their company and won't give a reason, except to say she has no patience, they talk too much. My sister thinks it is because she is having trouble remembering the rules of the canasta game, or that her incontinence makes her afraid to go out; I think it is more likely she has had another tiff with Lilly and won't admit it.

My sister sees her deficits and is constantly calling them to my attention; I see the still-vigorous qualities, and I fight back. They are both there, and neither of us can say which weighs more. It is a summer of careful observation and constant worry for my sister and me. Eight years and life-styles apart, ironically, it brings us closer together. Who knows what it does for my mother?

Sometime late in August, right before she is to return to Miami, she, my sister, and I are coming down the ramp of the boardwalk one day when my mother says, pointing to the sky, "What *is* that man doing up there?" We look at where she is pointing. Air and telephone wires. No man. We look beyond, for windows, for porches, for terraces, for cars, for low-flying planes. Anywhere a man could be visible. There is no man. There is a pair of sneakers tied together, hanging on the telephone wire. I squint and try to imagine how it can look like a man. Neither of us has the nerve to say, "There is no one there." Neither of us wants to confront my mother with the idea that she may be hallucinating. We want to avoid the idea, too. My sister says, "Mmmhmmm," and shakes her head, yes. I construct a man by superimposing the telephone pole with the wires. "It could be," I tell my sister, "if you don't have depth perception." I don't remember either of us connecting this to her story about her lost ring.

It isn't *quite* denial that makes these logical contortions. It is partly denial, of course, of the awful possibilities. But it is also part of the process of trying to figure out what is real in an unfamiliar world, in which the underbrush of fear and misconception and complicated emotional circumstance make it hard to see light. You know *something* is going on, but you don't know how to judge it. Fear inflates, fear obfuscates. You underreact, you overreact. In my correspondence and conversations with other people going through this, this is common. I know someone whose mother had Alzheimer's, and for three years, in the face of increasingly violent dementia, as long as the mother had the mind, at moments, to assure the daughter that she was "all right" and there was "nothing to worry about," the daughter could not see what was happening. I am a very observant person. When I read over my own catalog of "signs and omens" I ask myself how I could not have seen what my sister was seeing; or how my sister and I could have doubted that my mother was in serious decline. The answer is, I didn't want to see. The confusion comes from refusal to see. The image that keeps coming to me is "you have to clear the blood away." There was blood in my eyes, from the rupture of life as it ought to be. It is unnatural to tell your own parent what to do. Deciding mother doesn't know best anymore feels upside down, disloyal, and frightening as hell.

My sister and I talk about taking my mother for an evaluation but we don't know who to take her to. Neither of us have a family doctor we know well enough to talk to or trust. I get the name of a geriatric specialist, but we can't figure out how to get my mother there. I play out the dialogue but it all seems impossible. "We'd like you to see a doctor," we'll say. "Why?" she'll ask. I simply cannot supply the words that come next. And even if we could figure out how to get her there, we don't know exactly what we want of the visit.

Finally, I make a phone call to my mother's doctor in Florida. He has treated her for a long time and most of his patients are old. Maybe he can help us. (The words "help us" are about as specific as I can get my mind to be at this moment.) He tells me he thinks she is getting forgetful, and he informs me that she has had, over the past several years, some transient ischemic attacks, which amount to little shorts in the brain, ministrokes. I ask if these TIAs are something to be concerned about. He says no, but of course later I think the question is *can they be prevented?* All in all she is still in good shape, he thinks. As compared to what? I think. Terrific, he says. Quite a lady. He likes her. He approves of her spirit. I am relieved. I am proud that he likes her. But I don't have the nerve to ask him the one question that is poised and waiting in my mind: Can she still manage alone? Do we have to start thinking about taking care of her? I ask if he thinks she is getting enough nutrition, and he thinks not. He says he will recommend a supplement. I know my mother. She won't take it.

### Miami Beach, January 1989, Her Eighty-eighth Birthday

OUR flight lands at Miami International right on time and by noon we have our baggage and we're on the bus to the car rental terminal. The air is already humid, and the rental car door handle is too hot to touch. The way I like it. Not the way Marvin likes it, but since our bodies are still in shock, and New York was freezing cold, we drive the short distance down the coastal highway, lined with palm trees, up Arthur Godfrey Boulevard, to Miami Beach with the windows open, Marvin gasping in the warm, thick air, I gulping sentimental tears in anticipation of seeing my mother.

We pull up to the front of the apartment building on Collins Avenue, causing a flurry of excitement because the old people sitting in beach chairs outside the building know we are someone's kids from up north. My mother is not waiting, as she often is, and I have a moment of concern. We ride the creaky elevator to ten (the doors are deliberately slow to open and close, to accomodate the elderly tenants), impatiently. We lean on the bell. She answers as if she has been waiting behind the door, upset and delighted at once. She was, of course, sure we had gone down with the plane. She went upstairs to call the airline again. Why are we so late? Why didn't we call? She hugs me briefly but fervently, as if I have been reclaimed from the dead.

This is my favorite moment of the whole visit. When the hugs are done and the tears are dry, things usually go downhill. It always happens this way.

First, she will complain about our staying at a hotel

when she has a perfectly good place for us. (Of course, she doesn't, but she says it anyway. Her small studio sleeps two, and we are three, and though she *says* she will sleep at a friend's, this is not likely unless she can bring her own mattress.) We will want her to come with us to the hotel while we check in. She will refuse. Then she will refuse to come out to dinner, but will want to send *us* out. We will fight about it, and end up bringing food in and being mad because we had wanted to go out, and she will make some comment about whether it was really necessary for us to have bought the wine (calling it *likker*) which will drive us to pour another glass. Then she will insist upon paying for what we brought in, and we will fight about that and end up letting her pay, slipping the money into her purse sometime later. And then she will tell me to take home the gifts we and our kids and my sister and her kids have sent because they are too small or too big (she hasn't tried them on but she can *see*) or not the right color, or not the right style. The next day we will invite her to come and swim at our hotel pool, and she will say she has things to do, and for us to go on and have a nice "vacation" and she will see us later. I will fume "vacation!" and Marvin will take her at her word and get his towel and bathing suit, and then he and I will have a fight over it, and I will walk the eight or so blocks in the simmering morning heat to her apartment and keep her company while she does a wash or shops for groceries or takes me around to meet her friends. Over the past three years many of her friends have died, yet she always makes new ones, without comment. She has a kind of "well, that's that" attitude about it. The last time I visited, she took me grocery shopping. She shopped early in the morning, before the sun was high. She showed me the various benches, "sitting stops" she made along the route, so that she would have the stamina to do it. She was a strategist and a realist and proud of both. She talked often about her tennis past, as if this present strength owed something to that.

So she makes the hotel fuss, right on schedule, and refuses to come with us to check in. She gives the gifts a quick once-over and sends half of them home. But she is somewhat vague when it comes to dinner, so *we* suggest bringing food in. She looks even thinner than she did during the summer, and again, there is nothing in her refrigerator. She says it is because since she had a cold several weeks ago, she has not been able to go shopping. She paid a man who lives in the building to pick up some things for her, but there has been a hitch and now she isn't speaking to him. What's the hitch? He brought her things she didn't want, and claimed she told him she had wanted them; he said she gave him a five dollar bill, she said it was a ten. I automatically think she is wrong, and feel guilty.

Her apartment looks under the weather, too, in need of cleaning. The kitchen floor is sticky. The drapes are full of dust. And it doesn't smell fresh. My mother's secret (as she thinks) incontinence seems to have gotten worse. We have not been able to make any headway with her. She either denies it outright or gets so upset that we drop the subject. It embarrasses us. I keep trying to broach it. I give my mother the example of Mrs. B., an old friend and neighbor of mine who, at ninety-five, had the right idea: "Ooo," she would say, "look at that, I piddled. I left a little trail, like Hansel and Gretel!" and laugh and think no more of it than that. My mother gives me a look that says, "Oh, and I suppose you think that's just fine?"

Her laundry hamper is full, and she is wearing a stained blouse.

None of these things are like her, she who is so neat and clean she has been known to scrub floors at three in the morning just for the pleasure of it. When I ask about the woman who cleans her apartment, she says she has stopped coming. Then, a moment later, she says she let her go. She can't say why.

She needs Marvin to fix the television, which has been broken for months. He adjusts the color and it is fixed. (But this is an old story, my mother always maintaining the mystery of the electronics world, asking us to turn up the volume or change the channel as if it took some obscure knowledge.) On top of the television is a past due phone bill.

The next morning, I call my mother to tell her I am on my way to her apartment. We are going grocery shopping. Marvin will pick us up later, and we will all go out together. We are going downtown to buy a pair of sneakers. Since her fall, the only shoes she wears are sneakers and she needs a new pair. She still does not want to throw away the other twenty-nine pairs of shoes in her closet.

When I get to my mother's building, she isn't there. The desk clerk/handyman/doorman (a young West Indian whom she sometimes helps with his English lessons) says she has gone to meet me. "Where?" I ask. She didn't say. We didn't arrange to meet. We said I would come to her apartment. Has she somehow misunderstood? Have I somehow forgotten? I walked down on the boardwalk rather than the street, and I didn't see her pass me by. Have I missed her? Did she walk up on the street rather than the boardwalk? I feel alarmed, almost panicky, although it is broad daylight and this is her neighborhood. What am I thinking? Something about the heat of day. I ask the desk clerk if she was wearing a hat. Now it seems a silly question, like a neurotic mother fussing needlessly over her child. Do I say it in some sort of misdirection of my concern? What I do not say, or think, at that moment, even to myself, is that she might be confused, or she might not remember that I was on my way, or that she might forget where she lived and keep on wandering.

When I find her on the boardwalk, moments later, unperturbed, wearing a hat, she isn't clear about whether she went to meet me or forgot that I was coming, and when I press her, she says, "Oh, well, forget about it now, here we are," in her clipped, no-nonsense way. "Why aren't you wearing a hat?" she says.

The preceding autumn, when I had accompanied her back to Miami after her summer visit and she took me to the post office, we got lost; she said the post office moved. In that same visit she took me to the bank to add my name to hers and my sister's on the account. So at one and the same time, she refuses to admit her growing memory gaps, and yet she is making some kind of provisions. (Though there may be an additional reason for putting me on the account: She has recently become worried about money and this spring was convinced her accountant didn't file her taxes and she was going to jail, so my brother-in-law took over the taxes, and now she is worried about what my brother-in-law is doing with her money. I never mention this to my sister and who knows what my sister never mentions to me.)

We linger on the boardwalk, watching the tide. She keeps telling me, over and over, to go down to the shore and get my feet wet. She doesn't like the idea that we have come down here expressly to see her; it is too much for her to take—like having too much food in the refrigerator? She doesn't like people giving her things; she discourages gifts or returns them. I thinks she gets uncomfortable at the idea of wanting or needing something, as if it might compromise her independence. So she pushes this "vacation" we're supposed to be on at every turn. I say I don't want to wet my feet. She must tell me ten or more times to go down to the shore and wet my feet.

When we shop for groceries, I remind her that she likes ice cream. She used to be an ice-cream hound, I tell her, and she frowns, as if the figure of speech offends. She remembers, though, and agrees to let me put a small container in the cart. She wants only the smallest containers of everything, and gets angry and frustrated when I try to restock her pantry with staples and old favorites. Now, she isn't even interested in paper goods; she seems unsure of herself here, in the supermarket, where she used to whiz around, picking up bargains, knowing the brands, enjoying the process of selecting superior goods and rejecting inferior ones. Finally, I buy things surreptitiously, slipping them into the cart. She doesn't seem to notice then, or when I unpack them later at home.

When we go downtown, she balks at buying sneakers. She says she has plenty of sneakers. I remind her that she was the one who had said she needed sneakers, and she had showed me how worn her last pair was. She no longer loves being in a store, and on the contrary, seems bewildered and distressed by the abundance of merchandise on the shelves. I try to joke her out of it, and I say it is unheard of for her, the shoe nut, not to want a new pair of shoes. She laughs at my joke but we still come home with no sneakers. She is sorry that she has annoyed me, she says, but she doesn't want sneakers. Did she forget she needed them? Is she too depressed to buy something new? Is she afraid to spend the money? Her forceful will is certainly intact. She held me off firmly. And so what if she doesn't want new sneakers? If the old ones are good enough to still wear, why should I care? Maybe she just doesn't like me telling her what to do. I know I wouldn't want my kids to tell me what to do. I don't want to impose my will on hers.

And when I report to my sister, when we speak that night, instead of telling her about the morning's misdirections, the empty fridge, the odors, the mess, the main story is a funny one: How my mother has hidden all birthday cards and balloons that mention her age because she doesn't want anyone to know she is eighty-eight. She is passing for eighty-five. ("What is it anyone's business?" she said.) We laugh. Like the time she bawled my sister out for letting her hair go gray at the temples, because having a gray-haired daughter made *her* look older. Because this reassures us, this feels right. All the other stuff is a sidebar to this because in this my mother prevails, is "true to form," is as stubborn as ever, and is, above all, still herself.

I find myself judging her every act. She likes the watch we have bought for her birthday. She doesn't want me to take it back, or return, or exchange it. The watch *and* the band. A miracle. (Not like her.) It is the fourth watch in as many years we have bought for her birthday. She has lost all the others. (Like her.) She also lost or misplaced her diamond ring, gold bracelets, and a necklace. (Like her.) Someone might have come into the apartment while she was away, and stolen them, she says. She repeats this summer's wedding band story again. (Remembers it!)

"Who?" I say, but she doesn't answer.

Step by step, we are moving into the upside down world where daughters are mothers and mothers become the children. "You must have had a dream, mom," I say, tactfully.

My sister and I agree to take over the paying of my mother's bills. We split them up. I arrange to have her phone and rent bills sent to me. I tell her. I tell her it is because she is "absentminded," using a word I know she won't mind, because she has always been absentminded. Still, I am nervous, waiting for an argument, waiting for her to say, "I don't need you to do this, I can do it myself." To my surprise, she doesn't object. She almost waves it away, as if it is some minor arrangement, rather than the usurpation of her autonomy. "I've always been a little absentminded," she comments, and although this is what I had hoped she would think, still, there is a part of me that is shocked and disappointed. This is not like her at all.

Though we have come to this agreement, my sister and I are more in conflict than ever before. I see the taking over of my mother's bills as a "solution" to the "problem" of my mother. My sister sees it as another step (forward? down?). Or a sign. She wants to start looking into adult residences. I resist. She points out how many of my mother's social props are gone: She doesn't play cards anymore, she resigned as secretary of the building's social club, she has made no new friends since Lilly is gone, and she stays at home; I point out that she still keeps her beauty parlor appointment once a week, and has her nails done, and still talks about needing a good book to read. I decide she needs outside stimulation. I arrange to have the Miami Herald delivered. While my sister is trying gently to "close up shop" I am opening accounts for her. I draw a line in my mind: *not until she isn't herself* will I cross it.

It is the next day. She and I are sitting on the boardwalk. She is making sharp, critical comments about the people passing by. Things about people with fat behinds wearing hot pink shorts and hairdos that don't, and so forth. It's the kind of biting commentary I'm used to hearing from her, and ordinarily I would say "shhhh" and bite my lip and worry someone will hear her but this day I feel only relief. This is herself.

We have just come from her favorite shop in the basement of the Cadillac Hotel. It is slightly larger than a closet and stuffed with an array of sweatsuits in pinks, blues, and white, all with some kind of sparkle dust or sequined designs on them. She is dying to buy me something and I am refusing, and she can't see why. My sister liked them when she was here, she tells me, making the old sibling-rivalry maneuver. "What do you mean 'not my style'? Why do you always have to be different?" she says. This is a familiar old sweet song. She says it affectionately, and without vehemence, and I sigh, ritually and with some pleasure. In her eyes I am still a teenager. This is herself.

I am keeping her busy until Marvin can finish cleaning the floors. She refused to let us call a cleaning woman, or to take a hand ourselves. Were we saying her house was *dirty*? Of course not. (This is herself.) She finally lets me help her do the laundry, basket after basket, as I discovered that her closets and drawers, as well as the hamper, is filled with dirty clothes. (Not herself.) I have always been an obedient (though defiant) daughter and I feel disobedient now, sneaking around, cleaning up her house behind her back. While we sit there, companionable and calm, I try to talk with her about the incontinence again, but she claims the accident she had yesterday was the first of its kind, the very first. I do not have the nerve to dispute this with her. But I want to. I push the discussion forward anyway. I tell her not to look at it as a thing of shame, but as a simple muscular failure, and if she will just wear one of those Depends, it won't be a problem. She asks what they are, and I tell her, for the umpteenth time, avoiding the word *diaper* and she says of course she'll use them, why wouldn't she, they sound just great. I say good, I'll buy you a package, and she says no, not right now. "When I need them, though, they're good to know about." I feel like a hypocrite. I wish I could be as unperturbed about incontinence as I pretend. I try to desensitize myself. I try looking at the word dispassionately. Once, did I not know what it meant? Did it mean nothing to me? Could I have, because of its sound and the prefix, mistaken it for the word "inconstant," a word I might have read in a nineteenth-century novel, and which means fickle, as in "an inconstant lover?" It still reminds me of the word "inconstant" because an inconstant lover is a betrayer, and an incontinent bladder betrays its own body. That, too, sounds like it comes from an old romance, and it makes me think of the rash and incontinent lovers who cannot contain their ire or ardor. But of course, it prob-

ably comes from the same root as the word "contain"
and I know that it means inability to control the bladder or contain what is within. A bladder is only a container for bodily waste, I tell myself. I free associate. I say
words and phrases that I hope, once said, will lose their
power: *smell, loss of control, back to the diaper, bad girl.*
What if you lived on another planet, I ask myself,
where tearing eyes were frowned on instead of
untimely urination? You go your way, let society go
theirs, I scold. Better get over it, I warn myself, dropped
bladders run in families, and it will happen to you, too,
before you know it. I wonder if all those years of wearing girdles destroyed her muscles. I do Kegel exercises
and abdominals. I try to be like a friend who is defined
in my eyes by one act: When his mother was dying of
cancer, and she soiled herself, he bathed her and when
she apologized for the awful mess, he said, "You did it
for me, and I am glad to do it for you." I want to be like
that. But I can't. I am judgmental and disgusted and
embarrassed and I am sure my mother knows this is in
me as surely as she feels it in herself.

When we go upstairs, far from being angry that
Marvin cleaned up for her, she is delighted with what
he has accomplished. "Marvelous Marvy," she says, and
claps him on the back. We take her out to dinner, to
Al's, and she eats well. (Who am I to be pleased with
her eating?) We have coffee and ice cream in her apart-

ment. She enjoys the ice cream thoroughly. She is in a good mood. "Sit over here," she says, wanting to give Marvin the "good" chair with the ottoman. We watch TV. She gabs about her neighbors, wicked and funny. One talks too much; one, it's a shame, died; one is nice but stupid. I tease her about one of the widowers who used to be her cha-cha partner at the holiday parties. "Oh," she says. "Old men. Who needs them. They pee in their pants."

She tells us how Lilly, when they were taking her off to the hospital with a heart attack, called from the lobby wanting my mother to ride with her in the ambulance.

"Did you go?"

"At two in the morning? The nerve of her!" she says. I think "bitch" and am glad.

She can't get over what Marvin did. She surveys the newly-clean apartment with affection, as if for the first time. "Isn't this nice?" she says. "Now why couldn't you sleep here instead of going to that expensive hotel?"

We go back to the hotel feeling happy.

The next day is a disaster. It is raining and she seems like the weather. Foggy and overcast. I decide that she needs a treat, an outing. We decide to go to a big bright mall. Before we go, I try to tactfully suggest that she wear a protective pad. She agrees. She seems quiet, and inattentive, and when we get to the mall (The Avventura, one of those monster malls, in the upper reaches of

Dade County), she is uninterested in window shopping or even walking around. She is worn out, it seems, from the ride. She wants to sit down. She tells us to go ahead and we do, walking distractedly for half an hour. When we come back to the bench, my mother is nodding off, her head down. She looks like an old lady, one of those old ladies you see on benches, nodding off. It may seem strange, since she is eighty-eight, but I have never seen her like this before. I wake her gently, and though she is still a little fogged, we lift her up to go. The bench where she has been sitting is sopping wet. I am choking. I want to scream "What did you do? What did you do?"

I walk behind her, and we find a plastic bag to put on the seat of the rental car. We don't stop for lunch. We drive straight home.

In the lobby of her building, one of the sitting old ladies says, as she passes, "Mary, dear, the whole back of your pants are wet."

"Oh," my mother says, without missing a beat. "I must have sat in something! Thank you."

## Miami Beach, January 1990, Her Eighty-ninth Birthday

MY sister and I usually stagger our visits so that my mother can have two visits per winter instead of one;

this year, however, we have decided to go together.

As we pull into my mother's driveway, I see that the art deco restoration has finally reached this section of Collins Avenue; her building is newly painted, a bright pastel facade, and across the street the Cadillac is closed pending major renovations. I imagine pink flamingos, neon palms, the works. Lilly, who lived there, is temporarily living in the home of her nurse; but when her heart stabilizes she is going to California to live with a granddaughter. She will not come back to the newly-grand Cadillac.

Everything is changing. My mother's building management has made a new rule: Residents are not allowed to sit in front of the building. The chairs have been removed. A seating area inside is arranged for them. They are no longer visible to or from the passing cars. They don't fit with the new, hot scene, after all. I wonder when they are going to get squeezed out of this fashionable new world altogether. I wonder if, when it happens, it will affect my mother or if she will be in another place.

I have begun to consider the possibility that before long some change will have to be made. I am not sure how she is managing on her own. Our phone conversations show her forgetfulness is getting worse. Sometimes she calls because she forgot she called. At first this is funny. But the frequency of calls gets disturbing, especially for my sister, who gets the brunt of them. And my mother is constantly anxious now because she can't seem to hold in her mind for more than a few hours our reassurances about her bills being paid. Her worries center generally around money, where hers is (in the banks), which banks, who is paying her bills, why her pension check is late (we have arranged direct deposit into her account). She has nothing to worry about, but she worries. On the other hand, she does not worry about her health. We do. Is she eating enough? She will not discuss having any part-time help. We try. We don't say "aide," we say "maid" but she says no to everything. We have not thought it through. If she had said yes what would we have done then? We have agreed that her apartment is too small for anyone to live-in, and even if a move at this time were feasible in her shaky condition, we couldn't afford a larger apartment *and* live-in help. This birthday visit is unofficially an investigation. I think my sister and I want to be here together, to see it as one, and possibly reach a concensus. I feel bad. I feel like an enemy spy in my mother's house.

My sister has already checked in with my mother, and is waiting at her hotel to hear from us. We give my mother her birthday gifts: another watch (she took a bath with the one we gave her last year), some clothes, a pair of sneakers which my daughter has studded with rhinestones. She does not seem very interested. We call my sister at the Doral. We are staying a block away at the Fountainbleau-Hilton. We take my mother with us. She does not object. In the absence of her objection, I suddenly realize why she didn't like going there with us all those years. She felt it was "richer" than she, and she does not like to be anywhere that she does not feel superior to others.

She doesn't eat her lunch at the Fountainbleau, even though it is pizza, her favorite. She looks tired and distracted and her eyes are deeply circled. We talk around her and she sits and blinks in the sun. Later, we go to my sister's hotel suite and open a bottle of champagne to toast her birthday. It seems a very unfestive time, suddenly, but we had planned this and we don't quite know how to change the plans.

Later that afternoon, my sister and I talk. She is concerned by how out of it my mother seems to be. I argue that she has always been overwhelmed by occasions and that having the two of us (four of us) there is simply too much for her. But this time it's like I'm banging pots against the thunder. I am arguing because I agree with my sister, not because I don't.

The next day she brightens somewhat when my sister and brother-in-law bring my brother-in-law's father to the Fountainbleau for lunch. My mother has known Leon for a long time and is glad to see him. But he is not well. Now the two of them, after their greetings, sit and blink in the sun. It occurs to me clearly, when looking at Leon, that he does not quite know where he is. I wonder if it is possible to look at my mother with the same kind of clarity, and if I did, if that is what I would see. It is hot, and we move to the shade and order lunch: sandwiches, soda, and potato chips. My mother eats the chips and drinks a little soda. She sits patiently, emptied, it seems, of things to want or need, of things to do or make us do. We take her home when we are ready. When it is convenient. I wish she would make a little trouble.

## Miami Beach, March 1989

THIS morning G, my mother's neighbor, the lady with the Ed Wynn tremor in her voice, calls my sister. My mother has fallen again. This time she didn't pick herself up. G found her in her apartment, unable to move, at the foot of her bed, wet, shivering, and naked. G is not sure how it happened. My mother was not sure either. She said there was water on the floor and she slipped. She said she crawled to the door and opened it, and then crawled back and waited for someone to come. It is true; G found the door open. But why didn't she use the phone, which was closer? Why didn't she pull a blanket down and cover herself? She is not sure where she fell. Something about this does not add up and my mother is in no shape to re-add it. She has been taken to Mt. Sinai Hospital, where she is flat on her back with a fractured lumbar vertebra, but worse than that, she is in and out of her mind. Mostly out. She thinks she is at home, then she thinks there are people in her home; she has thrown them out but they won't go. She says, "What are you talking about, hospital?" She thinks all the women in white are from her manicure salon. She calls me, screaming, "Call the police, help me, call the police," because she is being held against her will and I am the only one who can save her.

She *is* being held against her will. They have put restraints on her, tied her wrists to the metal bars that are attached to her bed, because she won't stay put. When they try to tell her that she has an injury and will fall if she tries to walk, she says, "Nonsense." We hire a private nurse to watch over her, so that she does not have to be restrained. We speak to every nursing supervisor on every shift, but there is no way of being sure that she is not still held by the wrists, and the phone calls continue. We try to take care of her long distance, while we make plans to get down there. We speak with the doctor. He wants to get her into rehabilitation as soon as possible. Her confused state is probably a result of shock from the fall, and if it is, should clear shortly, the doctor says. If it doesn't, we are told, my mother will not be accepted into the rehabilitation program at the hospital. She is to be evaluated by the social worker in the hospital within the next twenty-four hours. She is evaluated. She fails.

Through her doctor's influence, she gets a bed in a nursing home/rehab facility nearby, in upper Miami Beach. We are grateful. We don't know where it is, or whether it is a snake pit or not, but the doctor makes it sound as though we are lucky and we ought to be grateful, so we are.

We are lucky. The rehab nursing home facility turns out to be clean, attractive, efficient. My mother is in a semiprivate room. Her roommate is a woman in her early eighties, with far more extensive physical problems than my mother, but with a clear head. I find myself wishing their conditions were reversed. My mother's mental condition has not improved. She is not sure where she is, and only sporadically remembers that she was moved. At this point, no one seems to expect things to change much for the better. The doctor feels that my mother can no longer manage on her own. We don't have to couch the question, and he does not hesitate or think about it for long.

When someone does not know where she is, but can still state positively that she does not want anything to eat and has the strength and will to refuse it, she becomes a "difficult patient." My mother is difficult. Though she excels at her physical therapy (she thinks it is a game; she wants to win them), she does not win friends on the nursing staff. Finicky as always, she does not like the food, and there is nothing the nurses can do—bully, coax, beg—to make her eat it. I know that nurses are generally overworked and underpaid and, despite that, a lot of them are patient and kind, dispensers of the tender loving care that makes healing happen faster. The nurses in this rehab, however, are neither kind nor patient. Tender, forget. (And maybe not even efficient, since they do not succeed in getting her to eat.) What they are is *mean*. They treat my mother with disrespect and even dislike. (Maybe they do dislike her. She is certainly not ingratiating.) They don't bother to even pretend kindness to her, not even in front of her family, and their handling is brusque and ungentle. And my sister and I find ourselves trying to be ingratiating in her stead, to make up for her, so that they will not be even meaner to her when we are gone. We take their side in the food wars, we scold her, we commiserate with them, we do battle with my mother over every morsel she won't eat. I don't really believe her life is in danger if she doesn't finish her omelet or eat her soup. I assume if her lack of nutrition were dangerous, they would have put her on intravenous feedings, but they do not. Nevertheless, the *tone* of the battle is at this pitch and I ignore what I know about my mother, which is that she can't eat, she is too frightened to be hungry, and her throat closes up when she is forced to do anything. That is how she is. I should come down hard on those nurses, tell them to leave her alone, that she is a grown-up of eighty-nine and if she doesn't want to eat, she doesn't want to eat. But I don't. I join those who tell her she is a "bad girl" for not tasting her rice pudding which the dietician has put in the little plastic cup just for her. This is the beginning of the end, right here. I see it and I don't see it. It is the beginning of tiny disloyalties in the name of her good health and well-being. It's tough *not* to take the valuation of others when they are experts. But sometimes you have to.

AT this point it is our impression (which no one dispels) that my mother's mental state is permanent. After the doctor's early expectation that her fog would clear does not come true, no more is said about it. This is a crucial point. I want to emphasize it because it illustrates the way old people are treated, in the medical establishment as well as out of it. If someone younger were admitted to a hospital and while there began to hallucinate and in other ways lose touch with reality, it would be expected that good medicine, aside from making sure it was not the fault of a drug or drug interaction, and speculating on the nature and shock of the injury itself, would include—once the patient's injury was stabilized—aggressively treating the mental condition. But because my mother is old, and known to be forgetful, the assumption (on all our parts) that this fall hastened her decline is not really questioned, and her mental state is not addressed except in the most perfunctory way. (The social worker in the hospital visits with her a few times, but it is my impression that this is more in the way of assessment than therapy.) And making the same assumption, egged on by the so-called experts, my sister and I act on the information we have. (You know what they say about elderly people—if they fall, they break a hip, if they break a hip, it's the beginning of the end, because they will most likely get pneumonia and die. You hear this so often it is like a proverb. Yet who would let some old person lie there without setting a broken hip, just because she was going to die anyway? Yet with this mental break, there is a subtle lack of interest, a too-quick acceptance of it as permanent.) Her confusion is accepted as inevitable and irrevocable. No drugs or psychiatric referrals are suggested. It is, plainly, not up for treatment. And on this small detail hangs my mother's fate.

My sister and I begin looking for a "place" for my mother. (This word, "place" is the operating euphemism we silently agree on; it protects us from facing what we are doing and it mutes the conflict between us.)

What we are doing, in looking for a "place" is sabotage. We both know that. Given who my mother is —independent, proud, with surviving intelligence—

making this life decision for her without her approval, agreement, permission, and deciding against what we know would be her own wishes, is sabotage. Yet, it seems necessary. I think we both believe that somehow, once we find a "place" we will come up with a way to get her approval. We have to. But we can't think about it now. It is obvious that the worst way to do this horrible thing we are thinking of doing is under a time constraint, but we have three weeks and then her time runs out at the rehab facility and they won't keep her beyond that.

The conflict: My sister believes that the right "place" is a Miami area Adult Care Living Facility (ACLF), a category of housing in the State of Florida which corresponded (at the time, the designation has since changed) to the Health Related Facility (HRF) in New York. It provides meals, cleaning services, communal activities, and custodial care when only minimal physical assistance is necessary; nursing care is on site, doctors on call. (In Florida, many of these are connected to nursing homes, so that when a resident deteriorates further, they can just move her to another building with a minimum of fuss.) My sister believes the move from rehab to the "place" should be local, as it will be less traumatic for my mother in her condition. She also believes the Florida ACLFs as well as the southern climate are better.

I am adamant. The only "place" I will consider is a senior citizen apartment house in New York, close to the two of us. I want to leave my mother as much privacy and autonomy as possible under the circumstances. I believe that if we get part-time help, and both of us and our families are close enough to help, we can pull it off. My fantasy includes Thanksgivings at my house, with my mother safely ensconsed, holding a baby on her lap. (Of course, at the best of times, in her *full* mind, this scenario wasn't real, and even as I dream it, I know that, but dreams die hard.) Most of all, I want to see her end her life without this compromise that any other "place" represents. My sister and I argue about our preferences, and it occurs to me we are also talking about ourselves, eventually. I'd want to preserve my privacy above all; my sister says, hell, what's so bad about having a built-in social life when you can't go out and get it? We do not argue that what we want is what will be best for my mother, nor that we are "going behind her back," and it makes us feel rotten.

We agree to each research our own preference. We spend days on the phone calling agencies and following leads and nights talking to one another. My sister's research reveals that the ACLFs in Florida offer much more than their counterparts in New York. She has brochures sent to me. I admit they sound good, some of them even idyllic. Still, I will not be convinced. I want my mother in a place of her own. I still feel I can rescue her from old age.

My research quickly reveals that in our immediate area (and I am determined that she will be close enough to both of us for daily visits), senior citizen housing is hard to come by. There are waiting lists for a few of the senior citizen housing complexes, and some of them are too expensive. It doesn't matter. My mother no longer functions well enough independently to even be considered. I contemplate lying to get her in. When I talk with an admissions person (if I get that far, if I am not immediately told there are no openings or the monthly costs do not discourage me from going further) I try to minimize my mother's disabilities. After all, what old person doesn't occasionally forget to take her keys, or turn off the stove? What old person doesn't have occasional incontinence? Lying, of course, is impossible, as I quickly learn. No one is going to accept my mother without a PRI (Patient Review Instrument), executed by a specially certified nurse, which assesses the level of care the elderly person requires, with a particular eye toward reimbursable services, and in many cases a personal interview.

I obtain the name of a geriatric counselor, one in a growing field who have combined social work, financial planning, and legal expertise for the aging.

On a drizzly weekday afternoon, my sister and I (with our husbands for extra "ears" and a whole pile of papers which sum up my mother's financial and public life: her

lease, her pension documents, her bankbooks and statements, her current bills) go to her small suite of offices.

The first thing the counselor says is, "You may be paying me, but I consider myself your mother's advocate,"
which impresses both of us. (I am thinking, "good," she'll
protect my mother from my sister, while my sister is
thinking "good," she'll knock some sense into me.)

The first day we spend almost two hours talking
about my mother, ourselves, our worries and fears, even
our guilt. It is an enormous relief for both of us. The
counselor dazzles us with the depth and breadth of her
knowledge of the field of geriatric care, and we both
feel that we have finally been delivered from our confusion. We begin to feel ready to consider our options.
And "our" options begin with her next question:

"What does your *mother* want?"

That's easy, we both agree. She wants to be left alone.

"Then work toward that," she says. "It's her life."
Reading it now, it seems pitifully evident that that is
where we should have started, but at the time it
bounced off the quiet, tasteful walls of her office like a
revelation. It is the first and most important decision to
make, and it is *really* in my mother's behalf. It feels that
way. It feels like an anchor, that we can come back to, if
we need to weigh other decisions.

Also that afternoon she provides us with a crucial
piece of information that we had not had before. She

tells us that it is quite common for a "hospital psy-
chosis" such as my mother's to clear partially or wholly
many weeks after its onset, as a result of being returned
to a familiar environment. "Why not bring her home?"
she says. With full-time help, for a while. Instead of
making any hasty decisions or putting her in a "place"
which may or may not be right for her, do what she
would want and see if she comes around. "Give it three
months," she says. At the very least, we will have had
that three months to do further research. At best, she
will be able to stay where she is.

We come out of her office elated, upset, angry. Why
didn't the doctor suggest this? Why didn't anyone else
in the hospital or rehab suggest this? *Why didn't we, ourselves, think of it?*

The expertise and the kindly but objective counsel
of this specialist is a turning point for us. My sister and I
come to the realization that we must work together for
my mother. Neither of us want to see her in pain, or
frightened, or losing it. But through our fear, we at first
delayed too long, and then almost leaped right to the
end, as if to get it over with all at once. Now, for the
first time, we see that we have options and we promise
ourselves and each other that we will go slowly and
explore them before we jump to any hasty conclusions
again. The counselor reinforced what ought to have
been self-evident. My mother has earned the right to

live any way she wants. So what if we are offended by the smell in the apartment. How often do we visit? If she isn't offended, and she is still safe and able to manage, with help, why not leave her alone? So what if her apartment is too small for live-in help on a permanent basis? We can still do it for a short time, and maybe work something out in the meanwhile.

We learn about the financial aspects of the choices we have available to us. (My mother's assets include a small amount of cash and her teacher's pension.) We understand that proprietary institutions run for profit and that we must therefore conserve enough to get her into a nursing home of our choice, if it comes to that, but that once she is in a facility, when the money runs out (as it eventually does, for most people) the same level of care is then picked up by Medicaid. Through this counselor, we gain access to the whole world of institutionalized care for the aged: lawyers, physical therapists, nursing registries, meals-on-wheels, and complete listings of all the different classes of residential care facilities.

We had our work cut out, but at least we knew how to go about it now, and at least my mother will be waiting in the wings, comfortable in her own apartment while we do.

Enter Kate.

Through a friend of my sister's who owns a nursing registry, we find Kate, a retired registered nurse and a widow. You have to see her. Slim, petite, coffee-colored; a beautiful, stylish woman with long salt-and-pepper hair which she wears in a thick braid down her back. She looks like a fifties' Hollywood version of an Indian maiden. She has a girlish swing to her hips. She wears denim skirts and wide-brimmed hats and big sunglasses and gorgeous turquoise jewelry. The men in the building suddenly all want to come and fix my mother's faucets.

She lives less than an hour's drive north of my mother's apartment but for the time being she sleeps in, six days a week. We hire a relief on Sundays. We rent a parking spot for her in my mother's building. We worry about how we will introduce her into my mother's life. We tell her it is just until she is "back on her feet" but we might have said nothing. She is not clear enough in her head to object.

From the first day she is home from the hospital, Kate has her walking, at first on a walker, up and down the long corridor outside her apartment, then to the boardwalk and back, then on the beach, soon without a walker. She bathes my mother, shops for her, cooks her three meals, cleans the apartment. Within three months my mother is not only back to where she was (forgetful but sane), she is better than she was. She settles back and lets herself be taken care of, as if some early memory of when she had live-in help has surfaced; she remembers to what manor she has been born. Under Kate's care and feeding, she puts on weight. Her apartment is clean, she is clean. But Kate is more than just a nurse; she turns out to be a companion, as well. They go out to dinner, to the movies, shopping for clothes. Kate nags her to buy new sneakers. She and Kate sit on the boardwalk and make snappy comments about the people who pass by.

In many ways they are alike. Kate is independent, intelligent, stubborn, a perfectionist. She tries to tackle the issue of my mother's incontinence. It causes tension between them. Both of them are very private people, and the close quarters begins to get on both their nerves. After several months, when my mother is getting around safely on her own, we all decide it will be best if Kate goes home at night after dinner and comes back after breakfast. My mother can make her own toast in the morning if she so wishes, Kate cooks the large meal in the afternoon and leaves my mother a cold supper which she can eat whenever she is hungry. This is an improvement. Kate is happy. My mother is happy. She seems to be able to manage with part-time help and things seem, for the first time in a long time, stable.

At mother's ninetieth birthday, she is still in her own place. This is cause for celebration. Marvin and I fly down and Kate makes a beautiful birthday dinner for my mother and for us when we arrive. The apartment is clean, and my mother is, too, and healthy looking, and everything seems wonderfully under control. My mother seems more herself than she has in a long time. She treats Kate like an old friend; she is open, humorous, and critical. I feel we have saved her from having to end her days in a "place" other than her own home. We take pictures of our celebration, of Kate and my mother on the boardwalk, of the two of them standing and laughing on the beach. It is a good time.

But after her birthday, the conflict between them seems to intensify. There is no question she has come to rely on Kate, yet she complains about her, too. She begins saying Kate hits her. And Kate calls and complains about my mother, that she is verbally abusive and is telling the neighbors that Kate hits her. We try to mediate, long distance. We tell Kate to ease up on the incontinence and cleanliness issues. We try to talk my mother out of her hallucinations. (We believe that is what they are. Yet we call the neighbors to investigate.) We tend to believe Kate, not my mother. Why? Well, we tell ourselves it is because my mother's accusations sound vague and inconsistent. She changes her story. She also sounds curiously unemotional about it; it lacks conviction. She doesn't sound really angry or frightened. On the other hand, Kate sounds terribly upset. But are these just cop-outs? Are we more concerned about keeping Kate happy than we are about keeping my mother happy? Because certainly we realize that losing Kate will most likely topple the whole shaky system. My mother's obsessions have gotten worse: mostly about money. She hooks into a certain idea, where her pension is going, for instance, or whether her rent is paid or not, and she can't seem to shake it loose. She makes innumerable calls, she cries, she becomes hysterical and our reassurances last less and less time. One day, she calls my sister thirty-three times in the same day because she has received a bank statement which she mistakes for a bill. Thirty-three times my sister says, "It's not a bill, its a statement, mom," and thirty-three times she says, "Oh, thank god, I didn't know that. Why didn't someone tell me before?" She doesn't sleep for worry. She gets more and more emotionally frail. Yet, she is still able to wreak havoc. Kate calls one day, at the end of her rope. This is it. My mother and she got into an argument and my mother almost throws herself out of Kate's car. Kate has to call her own doctor to increase her blood pressure medication. She is finished, she is leaving. I beg her to go out for a walk. She goes out. She comes back. My mother is sweet again. Kate decides to stay.

In May, we arrange for my mother and Kate to fly up to New York for my daughter's wedding. We book her into a senior citizen hotel in Long Beach, Long Island, and we tell the management there, and ourselves, that this is a trial to see if she likes it so we can make it a permanent move.

My mother and Kate arrive and we take them to the hotel. By that night, Kate is ready to go back home. She summons my sister. My mother is tossing clothes around the room. My mother apparently does not want to share a room with Kate and, in fact, has refused. The two of them are at each other's throats. My mother has either hit or threatened to hit Kate. Kate has gone off to walk the beach, to calm herself down. My sister calms my mother. Later, we beg Kate to stay. She stays. Now, in the dining room, one of the old ladies at my mother's table has called Kate a *shvartze* and my mother is offended on her behalf, so they are allies and friends again. Thank god, whatever the reason.

My mother looks beautiful at the wedding as my son escorts her down the aisle. She is in blue silk and sequins, her hair beautifully arranged, her face made up and set in her "company coming" pose: chin up, proud, smiling. She is tiny, and her eyes sparkle like the sequins on her dress. But she doesn't really know where she is, or why she is here. She smiles and makes the appropriate sounds when my friends approach and speak with her, and they all tell me how fantastic she is, how "with it" she is ("God bless 'er," the obligatory tag line, when anyone over eighty does more than breathe in and out); but I know, I can see, in those sparkling—glassy?—eyes and in the things she says that she doesn't know who they are. She keeps a sharp eye on Kate (stunning, serene, no evidence of yesterday's fireworks), as if she does not feel secure without her. After a while she is tired and we send her back to the hotel. She doesn't mind if she stays or if she goes.

We see them off a few days later and I don't know who we are more worried about. Kate looks like she is about to collapse. It seems clear that the conflict between them is only going to be resolved by Kate leaving. My mother gets too overwrought too often for this to go on, nor can we see Kate taking much more of it. The thought of getting someone else seems unlikely, considering how my mother can be. She has already sent away a Sunday night relief nurse whom she doesn't like. (The woman went. She had no choice. She didn't want to make my mother more upset than she already seemed to be. ) So if my mother still has this power to throw fits and affect the world around her, how are we going to bring another person into her home against her will? How, as a matter of fact, do we expect to convince her to go into a "place"? But as long as she cannot be counted on to take her blood pressure pills or remember that the stove is on, I have to agree that she is no longer up to living in a senior citizen hotel; I see that she needs more. And my sister finally agrees that if she has to live in that kind of "place" it should be near us, where we can visit often, and make sure that she is well taken care of. Yet neither of us can think of a way to get her to agree to it, and neither of us wants it, so, though we begin actively shopping for a "place," we agree to continue with Kate as long as the two of them don't kill each other.

We focus on two levels of care, the nursing home, and the Residential Care Facility. We get leads by word of mouth and from our geriatric counselor. We call, we visit. Some days we feel the pressure to find the right place immediately, when she and Kate are at each other's throats, or when her depression or anxiety seems worse. But then she rallies, and I begin thinking this shopping around is just a fail-safe, and we won't need it, and yesterday's terrors seem like an over-reaction. On days like these, my hopes are seamless with my belief; one day soon she and Kate will go out to dinner, and then to a good movie, and then she will come home, and lie down and fall asleep and die peacefully, before she ever has to live in a "place" other than her own home.

What do we look for? Since her health is generally good, we are not so much interested in the full medical services of a Skilled Nursing Facility. As a matter of fact, the hospital-like ambiance of such a "place" is exactly what we want to try to steer clear of. What we want is a "place" which offers some medical care and guidance, where she won't be disqualified because of her incontinence. We learn that the designation Health Care Facility in New York State, which offered some medical attention for ambulatory and incontinent elderly, is being phased out, but some of these facilities remain with the new name "residential care facility" (how to build a bigger, better euphemism?) which offers several different levels of care. We concentrate on these. We want a place close to one or the other of us. We rule out anything more than fifty miles or an hour in travel. We decide (and this is confirmed by others who have gone through this) that proximity is crucial. This is one instance in which the geriatric counselor does not agree with us, and we spend some time visiting facilities she recommends and ruling them out because they are so far away. Still, though it is time spent, it is not time wasted, because we get to know what to look for when we visit. Money is a big factor. One highly recommended "place" is ruled out when I call for an appointment and am told (kindly, but firmly) that if my mother does not have a considerable sum (the specific sum is mentioned) it is pointless to come and tour the facility, because she won't get in. It is not unusual to be asked the state of my mother's finances as well as what her disabilities amount to, over the telephone, before agreeing to set up an appointment for us to take a tour. We learn that some residential care facilities are "open buildings," which means that residents can, if they are still able, come and go pretty much as they please. This is what we are shooting for: someplace where my mother can go for a walk or get some sun on her face. Beside the obvious basics of cleanliness and comeliness, these two —proximity and an open building—are the two features my sister and I concentrate on. We visit one place that seems ideal. It is small, within half an hour's drive from both of us, homey, with a small, flower-filled patio, in a suburban neighborhood. In the lobby, a current-events discussion is going on. But the administrator who takes us on a tour does not think anything of barging in on a resident to show us her room, acting as if she weren't there (and though it's true she might not have been alert enough to know or care, that is exactly the point), and she yells at another resident for being afraid to go out of her room. We visit this place two more times, hoping the administrator had been in a bad mood that first time, but she is miserably consistent and so we do not pursue our application.

On the other side of the coin, we visit one skilled nursing facility where almost no one is up and walking. Yet the spirit of both staff and residents is clearly wonderful and the director so loving and caring, that we go back and visit again, even though we know that the level of debility is entirely too high and we wouldn't have a prayer of getting my mother to stay there.

In the spring, we visit a residential care facility (rcf) in Long Beach, New York. It is a stolid, six-story brown brick building which stands on a boulevard along the beach. A double row of angled parked cars is a center island in the wide street, and houses of red brick and stucco surround the Home, in its shadow.

It is set deeply back from the curb and along its width are circular bays with shrubs, and benches for the old people to sit and take the sea air. A driveway wide enough for an ambulance slopes steeply on two sides to the two-door entrance. A sign warns visitors to open only one door at a time; the wind coming off the ocean can be fierce.

A visitor's book is open on a table in the small vestibule; the middle-aged receptionist hardly glances up to see if I sign or not, and then buzzes me in.

Oddly enough, this casualness, this missing air of officialdom is what has prompted me to re-visit this one several times, with an eye to eventually visiting my mother here. (I still have a hard time with the words I need to describe what I intend to do with the "place" and my mother: "check" or "put" her "in"? "Enroll" comes to mind, as if it is a school. Yet I know that "commit" comes closest; for this will be an involuntary move.)

As I enter my name in the book, I look through the glass to my right, at the lobby. The old, mostly women, sit on benches and chairs positioned against walls and pillars and in conversational clusters. Under the SMOKING PERMITTED sign, a thin, white-haired woman in a wheelchair, with the crumpled look of someone who has had a stroke, struggles to lift a cigarette to her lips. Almost everyone, wheelchairs and walkers pointed, faces the open dining room doorway. The tables are set for six. As I am buzzed in, the smell of institutional food (which to me seems a combination of cabbage, sour milk, cheese, and tomato soup, though often it contains none of these) mingling with the cigarette smoke, tells me it is lunchtime.

My appointment with the woman from admissions is for noon, and as I wait for her to take me on the promised tour, I try to be observant. (I say *try* because what I really want is to head for the door. It is, by now, a familiar feeling. It is how shopping for a nursing home is: every step plodded through a sludge of guilt, uncertainty, distaste, and bitter hope. My sister and I take turns, and report to one another, which helps, but not very much.)

I observe that the furniture is dark tan vinyl, that the flat, pile-less carpet is chocolate brown with a floral pattern that reminds me of the Chinese rugs that were in all the foyers of all the homes I ever lived in with my mother. I observed phone booths, soda and snack machines, a water fountain, a bathroom.

The three elevators open and close again and a procession of old people wheels, hobbles, or walks slowly in to lunch. Women outnumber men. Pink-uniformed aides come and go, some helping with the lunch detail, some on their way somewhere else. Everyone seems to know everyone by name, and when the woman from admissions finally arrives, and she too greets the residents by their first names, with easy friendliness, I think what an improvement this is over the last place I visited, where the seventy-five-ish director-owner called all the residents "dear" and managed to patronize and ignore them at the same time. (When he called me "dear" too, I made a silent prayer that one day soon he would get to occupy one of his own rooms.) Here, my spirits lift.

I see again today two representative floors (and the *floors* impress me: on one, plush carpet, on another, clean and impressively glossy wood-toned vinyl. The rooms, single and double, are cheerful, the walls covered in ugly-homey flocked wallpaper; the simple dresser-mirror-wardrobe-chair suites are individualized with afghans, flowers, stuffed toys, mementos, and pictures that residents are encouraged, I am told, to bring. The beds, with some exceptions, are not hospital beds, and what I think of as the usual nursing home smell—a combination of human waste, medicine, and Lysol—is barely detectable.

I see the auditorium, which serves as a party room and as a chapel, and separate dining facilities on some of the floors where it is hard for residents to get to the main dining room. There are sunny dayrooms that look out on the beach and beyond. I am struck by the fact that this view is almost exactly my mother's view from her apartment in Miami Beach. It crosses my mind that she could come here without feeling like she is going into an institution at all; in fact, for a moment I feel hopeful that the whole move can be accomplished without the phrase "nursing home" ever coming up. I feel like my mother's kid again, trying to "put one over on her," as if this is like hiding my string beans behind the potatoes so I don't have to eat them. Neither my sister nor I have yet been able to raise this matter of custodial care with her openly; we talk, obliquely, about "bringing her closer" to us, to a "place" which will include meals. But that's as far as we get: she stops us, saying she is comfortable where she is and to leave her alone. She is no dope. She knows very well, and we know she knows, but none of us have said out loud that this move means someone will wake her and wash her, that there will be no locks on her door, no keys to misplace, no laundry to do, and no groceries to buy. Dependence.

As I begin to like this "place" I begin to get tense. I am aware, either because of the woman from admissions' manner, or by my own sudden desire to have my mother accepted here, that admission is not secure. Nursing homes (and rcf's) are businesses, and today it is a seller's market; beds are filled and applications are up. So, though I started out thinking I was interviewing the nursing home, I see now that the nursing home

is interviewing me. I hear myself trying to "sell" my
mother: this prodigy oldster, with a strong mind, a sense
of humor, no diseases except old age and a tendency to
forget and a teensy bit of incontinence, a woman the
woman from admissions would herself want to know,
who will be an asset, who will be no trouble. Ridicu-
lous! I see the woman from admissions listening to me
with evident sympathy and no interest at all; she has
been through this how many times before? And she
understands, of course. And of course none of what I
think of as my mother's "qualifications" matter one bit.

What does matter? Briefly, broadly, how many beds
they have, how much money she has, and whether her
disabilities match the facilities of this Home; I don't
know in which order.

My mother has a nest egg, a pension, and her social
security. This is enough for an application. (When her
savings runs out, Medicaid will pay what her pension
and social security do not.) Since this "place" has a combination of skilled and support nursing care, and my
mother's disabilities (the frailty, incontinence, and loss of
memory) are mild but measurable, she fits. If the application goes forward, both the medical (that Patient Review
Instrument) and financial facts will have to be certified,
after which there will be an interview. I tell the woman
from admissions that my mother is frail and old and lives
so far that it will be impossible to fly her up *just* for an

interview. (I am wondering how we can get her to come at all, much less submit to any kind of interview!) I am told the interview can take place on the day she is admitted. But what if she "flunks" it after the arrangements have been made and she is already here? If the paperwork is in order, the woman from admissions assures me, the interview is a formality. (I wonder if this "paperwork is in order" is a euphemism for the check clearing.) The interview cannot be waived. It is to make sure my mother is in the condition we say she is in, that she is aware she is being admitted, and that she consents to it.

I think, "She will never consent," and of course what follows: How can I be doing this to her? How will I ever get her to *let* me do it? I am drenched in a tidal wave of fear, guilt, and sadness. I think of the enormity of the tasks before us: amassing the documents of her life, shifting her financial accounts, closing her apartment, moving her to New York; but most of all, of figuring out a way to tell her she can no longer live alone, that we, her daughters believe this about her, and—worst sabotage— make *her* believe it. And finally swallow it ourselves.

My stomach is in my throat and I am in a cold sweat. I want to get up and leave and never come back. I want to tear up the papers, and keep it the way it is, this jerry-rigged, cut-and-paste, hope-for-the-best, day-to-day, minute-to-minute life she (and we) lead now.

Then I remind myself why I am here in the first

place. And that this is the best home I have seen, a livable option. (That's what I asked for in my mind: a livable option.)

It is not a locked building; she can go out for a breath of air on her own.

She will be in a town where she once lived happily.

She will even have her beloved view of the horizon, as if we had packed it up and brought it from Florida for her.

She will be close to us, and if she falls, someone will be there to pick her up.

I swallow until my stomach goes back where it belongs, and I take the papers, and I smile, and I say, "See you soon."

## Miami Beach, August 1991, Hurricane Andrew

By the time we realize the storm is serious, we cannot reach my mother. Either the circuits are busy, her line is busy, or the phone lines are already down. We reach Kate in Hallandale. She started out, but was turned back by the police. They have closed the roads to Miami. She is, herself, refusing to be evacuated, preferring to stay safe (or not safe) within her own four walls. This is what my mother would wish, too.

For forty-eight hours, it is impossible to reach anyone

in Miami. Kate's phone is out now, too. We watch the TV news coverage. Safety instructions. Evacuations. Mounting damage. People nailing boards, boards blowing away. I stare at the footage of people seeking shelter, hoping and not hoping to see my mother. I do not know whether she is alive or dead, but I imagine her alive and frightened, caught in the wind, lifted and blown somewhere. She is barely a hundred pounds now, a wisp.

All at once, all the muddy wanderings and wonderings of the last three years, about whether or not she can manage on her own, are cleared away as easily as trees in that wind. I see her, without Kate, frightened and confused. I see her unable to find a telephone, unable to remember a phone number if she does. I see her oblivious to the images on the TV screen, which are telling her to seek safe ground. I see her answering the door for one of the maintenance people in her building, being told to evacuate, closing the door, and forgetting anyone told her anything. I see her the only tenant left in the building. Leaving the windows open. Getting blown out the window. Getting hit by broken glass. I think of the heavy mirror above the lime floral tub chair and I pray she doesn't sit in the chair. I see her evacuated, losing touch with her neighbors in some large armory or Red Cross shelter with nothing but strangers. In her right mind, her pride would not let her ask for help, especially from strangers. But maybe, if her life were at stake, she might have, if she had a mind to. Now, she can't. For forty-eight hours, all I think about is what "managing on her own" really means.

When the phones are working again, I reach the Dade County Police. It takes two hours to get through, but finally, someone is able to tell me that my mother's building has been evacuated; though of course they don't know if any of the thousands of short, blondish gray-haired ladies they have seen to safety is my mother.

When the worst of the storm is over, and the news broadcasts show people returning to their homes, I am still getting no answer by telephone. My sister is away on vacation, and is calling me every few hours to find out what is going on. I have nothing to tell her. Finally, I reach Kate, who has been able to reach one of my mother's neighbors. The last this neighbor saw of my mother was when she was being taken to a hospital. Why? She doesn't know. What happened? She only knows that there was "some problem." She doesn't know what hospital she was taken to.

Kate and I begin calling local hospitals, first in Miami Beach, and then in a wider area. Neither of us have any luck. The first effort is to get through at all with the downed lines and the busy signals. Once I get through, I say, "Hello, I'm looking for my mother." I try to describe her before they tell me that she isn't there; I can't just give them her name and count on that. What if she didn't remember her name? What if she gave them her maiden name? I don't want to hear that she isn't there, so even if they say she isn't, I try to engage them, to get them to take my number or Kate's, to call one of us if someone with my mother's name or description should turn up. They are inundated, they can't help me. I want someone to say, "She's here, she's safe," not, "The computer doesn't show anyone of that name being admitted." Half the time they cut me off, because I won't let them tell me no.

Kate begins calling all the neighbors in the building, hoping she can find out who knows which hospital my mother was taken to.

Reports of damage, confusion, and loss keep coming in, and the busy signals and the disconnects and the "not heres" continue. We wonder if we will find her at all. But we can't stop trying, and we don't know what else to do.

Many hours later, in desperation, I begin re-calling hospitals I have already called, in case someone has overlooked her the first time. I nag a harrassed telephone operator at Jackson Memorial until she finally rechecks her records. There *is* someone there with my mother's name, in the emergency room, she tells me. But she doesn't know what is wrong, what her condition is, and she can't put me through to the emergency room.

I call Kate and tell her. She wants to go there, but I tell her to wait until I can make sure it is my mother. I call my mother's doctor. He isn't there. I wait impatiently for him to return my call. When he finally does, an hour later, I tell him where I think I have found my mother and ask for his help. It is an astonishing stroke of luck; his son, also a doctor, is in charge of that very same emergency room, and he is able to get me through.

It *is* my mother. She's there. She's got a bruised arm but she is all right. The nurse who answers brings her to the phone to speak with me. I am overjoyed to hear her voice, which sounds a little annoyed at being called to the phone. She is fine, she says, why wouldn't she be? It's just that the damned doctor's office is so crowded with patients she's been stuck there for more than an hour! And how had I known she was going to the doctor this afternoon anyhow? In other words, she has no idea where she is, or about the hurricane, the evacuation, the ambulance ride, or how she has gotten the minor injury to her arm that has brought her there. She has no identification, and has not been able to tell anyone her address or phone number. Kate comes to take her home. It is clear. She is no longer herself. It is time to act.

## Long Beach, September 1992

SHE arrives on an early morning flight with Kate. We meet my sister and brother-in-law at a diner near Long Beach for lunch. We don't want to be late for the interview. We have not yet been able to bring ourselves to tell my mother that we are putting her in a nursing home. (What do we think she thinks?) We have no idea how this is going to play out. We are terrified. Even if she agrees to this "place" (we have told her we found her a "place"), what is going to happen if she has to share a room with someone? She will never agree. My sister and I know this. We have played this down to the wire, and now it is going to blow up in our faces. How is it possible for two grown women to behave so irresponsibly? Neither of us has slept.

She, on the other hand, is in a good mood, after an awful night according to Kate. She had refused to come, said she wasn't getting on a plane to anywhere, and if we tried to make her, she would jump out the window. Now here she is, telling Kate what to order, *remembering* that the specialty of this diner is its grilled cheese sandwich and the french fries are crisp and fresh. She does not ask where she is going, and when we get to the nursing home she does not ask any questions. I want to sprout wings and fly up and cover the sign which says, ". . . Facility" over the door. She doesn't give it a glance. Yet, while Marvin and my brother-in-law go for a walk, and Kate and my sister go to find the director, my mother and I sit in the lobby and wait. A wheelchair-walker brigade comes out of the dining room. My mother raises her eyebrows as if to say, "What a bunch," then observes aloud how many women there are.

"They live longer than men," I say. She nods. There is a small silence, and then she says quietly, "The trouble with a place like this, you get accustomed to letting them do things for you and next thing you know you can't do them yourself."

I can't answer. These are the words of my mother, not the words of someone lost to age and senility, who doesn't know where she is going. How much more does she know and not say? And with all that's lost, how much is left, and how, with what is left, will she resign herself to this?

We are kept waiting a long time, but there is nothing we can do. She is here, clothes, belongings, intentions, and it can't be undone. She has already forgotten the morning flight. She has forgotten that home is Florida, that this is New York, that she is moving from one to the other. (Though she knows she is waiting for someone, and keeps saying, "I'll give her five more minutes and then we'll go.")

The interview takes place two hours late, and aside from that, two unexpected things happen. After about twenty minutes, the director asks my mother to wait outside and invites my sister and me in. She is grim. She (not very delicately) probes us regarding my mother's incontinence; it seems my mother denied it and the director thinks we have lied. (This is important, because if we have lied, it will mean that we are trying to "dump" our mother here without regard to qualifying disabilities.

And if there are no qualifying disabilities, *physical ones,* then she will not be eligible for Medicaid when her money runs out.) We assure her of my mother's incontinence. (How far we have come!) She visits with my mother a few more minutes, and then calls us in again. She informs us she is placing her on Five, the floor reserved for patients with Alzheimer's and senile dementia. Neither of us speak. I can hear my sister breathing. This is the only floor in the building which is locked. I think *she will not be able to go out and get air.* She will be lost among the *really* senile and what will happen to what is left of her now? One of us says something in "defense" of my mother. The director is firm. She explains gently. She fears my mother may wander away, or be treated badly by more able residents on other floors; surely intelligent daughters will see this? She tells us a little cautionary tale about just last month when two not-so-intelligent daughters did not heed her advice and their mother was the sorrier. Old people can be cruel, she explains. In this other woman's case, she was ridiculed and ostrasized by others on her floor, and even then, to the very last, her daughters refused to understand, but finally they did and they admitted what she was now sure we would see: that this placement was for their mother's own good. My mother, she fears, will get lost on the elevator. There is a confusion in my mind. Did we "defend" her hard enough? Did one of us ask if we could give her a try on another floor with more able people, and *if* she got lost or wandered away or was treated cruelly, then we could move her to the dementia floor? Did we let ourselves be tricked by the director's appeal to our reason, tricked by our own desire to be calm? Because inside I was not calm, I was screaming. Did we fear that there were no other rooms and we would have to take my mother, truly confused now, into one of our homes? And for how long? Did we feel that, with no other places as "perfect" as this one, that we dare not ask for anything? Was it because the room on that floor was a single, and at least my mother would be able to still have her privacy? What kind of privacy were we think-ing of on the floor for senile dementia? This moment radiates in both our minds; it does not settle in the days and months and now years that follow, and I don't think it ever will. We have talked of it often. It is the moment we gave her up, the moment we truly "put her away."

Stunned, we take the elevator to that floor and walk along the long, clean corridor until we reach the room which is now her home. My sister and I do not look at each other. At least it's a single, one of us says. All of us help her unpack. Kate has brought some of her favorite knickknacks from her apartment. Kate fusses over them, and puts her clothing in the small dresser and hangs them in the wardrobe. We put her suitcases on the top of the wardrobe.

She is tired and dazed. It is nearly dinnertime and a

nurse brings her a tray for tonight, but she can't eat. We coax her to have some bread and butter and a cup of tea. I imagine the lump in her throat. How will we leave her here? How will she stay? ("Leave it to us," the director has said.)

A recreational therapist comes in. She is a large, pretty woman with a decidedly bouncy personality. She has a questionnaire. "Do you like games?" "No," my mother says. "Crafts?" "No." "Parties?" "No." Down the list, "No. No. No." Finally, laughing, the woman says, "Well, Mary, what *do* you like?" and my mother says, "Tennis." Then she looks up and smiles and puts out a hand to the therapist, as if to say she sees how hard she's been making it, and says, "I'm a little superior."

"I can see that," the therapist says.

MY sister and I argue. I want my mother to have a telephone. I want her to be able to contact the outside world. My sister doesn't. When I call to arrange for a phone, I am gently and indirectly discouraged. They tell me that it is, of course, up to me, but often residents who no longer have a conception of day and night call their children in the middle of the night. I know this is true. This is what she did to my sister. I say, "That's OK, I don't mind," but it will be my sister whom she will call. I don't arrange for the phone, and I feel awful about it. It takes her about four months before she stops talking about having a phone. Still, she calls. At first, I give her change, and she escapes and goes downstairs to the lobby to call from the phone booth. (She finds her way back up by herself perfectly well.) Sometimes a nurse or aide goes with her. After a while, after six months or a year, she no longer goes by herself, but they let her call from the floor desk.

*Miami Beach, October 25, 1992,*
*Breaking Up, Closing Down*

THIS weekend, closing up mother's apartment, raises some thoughts.

1. A whole life can be reduced to the contents of two plastic bags and a binocular case.
2. A modest proposal: Why *not* issue suicide pills? Arguments against it: they can be used by unscrupulous people for nefarious purposes—and an answer: the government can regulate as tightly as they do other prescription drugs. Who am I kidding? "Take me out and shoot me" is a movable conviction, always one step away, as far as I can see. She has long overtaken "If I ever get that bad" and she's worse, yet she doesn't want to die. I don't think she does. Why not issue the *right* to issue suicide pills? Then maybe

everyone would be happier to live on, in the knowledge they don't have to. This is Kevorkian's idea, too.

3. I always thought of middle age, like middle class, as a stop between one place and another. It always implied passage or progress from and to. But lately I can only think of it as a tight spot, a place between the freedom of youth and the demands of age. I'm stuck here. The mush in between my children and my mother, the filling in the sandwich, my time, my needs, squashed, oh, screw the metaphors.

4. When my sister says, "It's only possessions, inanimate things" she is quite right. But of course that is not the whole story. They are inanimate things that meant something to someone who means something to me. What did they mean?

The furniture bore the weight of her body and those of her loved ones in different times. The lime floral tub chair she liked to sit in, the "man's chair" with the ottoman, the only piece of furniture from the days of daddy; the gold sofa I slept on when I flew down to bring her up to New York. Their inanimateness now is the result of lack of use; stress and use marked them before. And the stuff—dusty beaded flowers she made in a crafts class; needlepoints from her needlepointing phase; afghans started by her and finished by the neighbor down the hall (but passed off as her own); vases and

teacups with floral motifs that everyone in her generation thought of as elegant, and everyone in my generation thought of as fussy; trivets from bazaars; potholders
and wall plaques made by grandchildren. Pictures, pictures, pictures. Everything looks dusty, junky, old.

Shopping lists, bank statements—reminders of a life
that no longer pertains—the sweetness of everyday com-
petence—to feed, clothe, and care for yourself—gone.

Letters from daddy—love gone.

Letter from the Parks Department on her tennis
medal, presented in a ceremony presided over by the
great Bill Tilden. Pride in skill and achievement. The
skill went; now the pride is still there. Will the pride
stay till the end?

Daddy's patent drawings. Pride in his invention. A
surprise.

Without someone to note them, they are garbage.

So my taking them with me is in respect and honor
to her *whether or not she knows it.*

Boy, that line from *Death Of A Salesman* really rings
today. "Attention must be paid." His wife Linda said it. I
am paying her attention, whether or not she can know
it. It has to do with respect. It has to do with what I
would want done for me. It has to do with the way I
want to be human. It is not quite my mother's way.

I am thinking all the way back to when Mom and
Dad used to come up from Florida.

Then Mom alone, walking athletically up the ramp.

Then Mom alone in an airline wheelchair, able still but taking the freebie offer, because she's a bit tired.

Then Mom in an airline wheelchair with me or Marvin pushing from behind.

Then Mom with Kate.

We call St. Vincent de Paul, and offer them everything. But they tell us that they will only take what they need, or what is of value. I feel insulted for the moment, that anyone would think these things of my mother's life are anything but valuable. I tell them they either take everything or nothing. They agree and when they come they seem pleased and assure us that such beautiful stuff as my mother's will be appreciated by the family who is getting it, who had been wiped out in the hurricane. It helps to hear this.

Kate's car isn't running and she has just gotten over pneumonia but she comes down by bus to help us. We give her a chair for an elderly friend of hers, and one or two small mementos of my mother. We drive her home. Her apartment is very different from my mother's, yet very much the same in its pride of place. She has mementos, we notice, of other former patients. She points out one or two to us. We embrace and promise to keep in touch. We go back to Miami Beach to finish up. St. Vincent de Paul has taken everything. There is really very little left to do. Marvin cleans up a bit, while I sit on the floor in the corner of the living room going through the last box or two of papers. My mother saved everything. There are scraps of paper from thirty, forty, fifty years ago; there are deposit slips and bankbooks from accounts long closed; there are some surprises, some personal things. While the charity people were taking things out, I decided to keep the picture that hung over my mother's sofa, not so much because I liked it, but because it seemed so much a part of my childhood. It had hung over the piano in our apartment in the Bronx, and I had practiced my scales by staring into the scene, to the disappearing road that went down the center of it. It reminds me not only of my scales, but of my mother, forcing me to practice, and my early dreams of escape, down that narrow road. The frame and matting are warped and smelly from water damage—my mother left the windows wide open during the hurricane—and I had twice hesitated, twice changed my mind about taking the picture. I do this with a lot of things; as the charity people take something, I hold it back, then let it go. In the end I take the picture and detach the frame, cutting away most of the matting. I place it between two towels and later lie it flat between layers of clothing in my luggage. I bring my sister one item as a memento. I throw away more than twenty pairs of shoes.

# PART TWO

# *Her Last Home*

*"What was the best time of your life?"*
*"When I was young, playing tennis."*

## Long Beach, Summer, 1993,
## An Extraordinary Conversation

I sit beside her in the sun. Her hand rests in mine. Her eyelids droop; it is late morning and the exertions of waking, eating breakfast, walking to the elevator, riding down, walking the short distance from the elevator to outside, and finding a bench have taken their toll on her ninety-two-year-old body. I rub the very smooth skin of her hand with my finger. Her eyes open wide and the pupils focus.

"Tell me," she says. She turns her face to me, the light of interest in her eyes: "Is mama alive?"

"No."

"And I suppose papa is dead, too?"

"Yes."

This is the third time today she has asked these questions. I could explain again that her parents are long dead, and those particulars of time which she no longer understands, that her mother would be one hundred fifty-six, her father, one hundred sixty. If I did she would repeat, "Really!" with a kind of mild surprise, as if to say those numbers impressed her, or that I had said something clever.

I ask her, instead, to tell me about her mama. I do this because I know the social workers think it's a good thing to do and I hope it will animate her; I also do it because there are things about my grandparents I want to know and my mother, in her full mind, did not reminisce, never had the patience or temperament for it. (I feel sneaky, getting her to do something she would not have done, once.)

She says, "Oppressed. I think she was . . ." She flounders, her mouth opening and closing rapidly, she stutters, looking for syllables she has lost. "Held under papa's thumb," she says, finally. She is losing language, yet she still makes subtle choices, and she hangs on tightly to the thought, reaching hard for the right word. You can see it in her face, which strains, as if the mental effort is physical, as well.

I smooth the hair from her forehead. The hair is pepper and salt, mostly salt now, thick and wavy, and cut short. Casual, the way I like it. When I was young, hair was a bone of contention between us. Mine was never neat enough. She pulled it into braids, pushed it out of my eyes, tortured me with permanent waves, while I mocked the fact that she went to a beauty parlor once a week and came out with an immovable head, puffed up and lacquered stiff, around which she wrapped toilet paper at night to preserve it while she slept. It was a matter of values, hers a deep belief in order and following rules, mine about wanting to break them. But as mother and daughter we didn't talk that way; we took it out on each other's hair. Now, my sister and I arrange for her to go to the nursing home "beauty parlor" once a week, and she refuses.

I touch her cheek; it is papery smooth. When I was a child, we never touched. She was not affectionate, and I was usually too mad at her to try. Now, there is license in my caress and license in her acceptance of it. Her eyes get teary. She thanks me for a wonderful day. (We have been together half an hour.) She says it is kind of me to come and waste my time when I must have things to do. Once, I would have taken this as sarcasm, aimed at letting me know I don't visit enough. That would be the mother I once knew. The mother she is now means it. But she will also not remember, tomorrow, that I have been here at all. When my sister visits in a day or two she will ask, "Do you ever hear from Bette?" as she has asked me twice today if I ever hear from my sister.

"I'm ready to go up," she says, and gives me her arm. She holds on tightly. I remember how daring she used to be, crossing streets. To catch a bus on the other side, she would grab me by the hand and step into traffic, and with the other hand hold all the cars back.

Before we go up, we walk to the corner, about forty feet. My mother says it is good exercise, though it exhausts her. It always surprises her how exhausted she becomes, because once she had an athlete's stamina. "Look at me," she commands. "Mary the tennis player!"

In the elevator we meet one of the recreational therapists, who greets her exuberantly.

"Mary, are you going to come dancing this afternoon?"

My mother blushes and smiles. "I don't know," she says.

"Mary, we need you," the therapist coaxes.

As always, I am torn between gratitude at the cheerfulness and annoyance at the patronizing tone.

But my mother, who used to be a pretty good shit detector, seems to take it in stride today. "Well, alright, if you need me, you need me," she says.

(I try not to, but I can't but help think of it as decline for her to take it in stride; during her first month here she challenged someone using her first name, saying to her snappily, "Do you *know* me?" and once, when someone asked her a stupid question, she glared and said, not answering, "You'll have to excuse me, *I'm* used to asking the questions.")

I walk her to the dining room, where lunch is about to be served. Paper setups are on the tables, and my mother's tablemates sit waiting, their heads bowed in sudden sleep, or stupor.

"Mary," the nurse says. "Did you have a nice outing?"

I kiss her goodbye. She thanks me again and I say, "See you tomorrow," though I know it will be a week before I come again. This is cheating, to make her happy for the moment I say it, or to make me a better daughter for the moment, in her eyes.

It has been a good visit. Yet, as always, I am relieved to drive away, and sad.

"This is a good school," my mother said after the rec therapist left the elevator. "The teachers are friendly."

". . . a good home," I tell myself. But then I think, as my mother once said, "Shoot me first."

## Five, The Dementia Floor

AT one end is the dayroom, at the other, the dining room. Three elevators open in the middle and as you step off, you face the nursing desk and behind it the nursing office, where you can find the two floor nurses, and where the files and medication are kept.

The rooms, singles and doubles, line either side of the long corridor, and against the walls are large, compartmented wagons of waste and diapers, dirty laundry and housekeeping materials. Cleaning is always going on on Five.

There are no locks on the large, solid wooden doors, and beside each doorway is the door number and the resident's name. In this way, Five is the same as all the other floors, except not all floors have their own dining rooms.

But here, the similarity ends.

On Five, there is no carpet. The floor is shiny wood-patterned vinyl. I remember admiring it when I visited. The reason there is no carpet, I realize now, is that toilet accidents here are so common.

Old age on Five is not cozy. In the realm of the senses, it is rich. Sometimes you smell it first. Then you hear it. Screech, moan, chatter, whine, cry. If you step off the elevator just as everyone is tuning up, it sounds like the orchestra from hell.

What you may see, as you walk quickly down the aisle (and you do want to walk quickly, eyes front, head down—yet at the same time you can't resist staring) at various times is a granny or two in crash helmets; a young-looking woman clutching a stuffed animal against her breast; a wild-haired, wild-eyed woman lurching down the hall straight at you on a walker, begging you to take her home; a roly-poly woman who holds out her arms to you because she thinks you belong to her; someone with her trousers around her knees, trying to make it to a bathroom; one of the usually two or three men on the floor, this one walking aslant, so he looks like he is going to fall over backward. To an occasional visitor it can be unsettling and disturbing. If you visit on a regular basis, you find it is also colorful, crazy, heartbreaking, and even funny.

What is "life" like on Five?

By "life" we usually mean a combination of day-to-day chores and some larger sense of purpose. On Five, all of those chores of day-to-day living are now taken care of by nursing aides, each of whom is assigned to a group of residents. As my mother predicted on that first day, when you let other people do things for you, you forget how to do them for yourself. People on Five have forgotten about cleaning, cooking, serving, dressing, being mistresses of their own homes. (Though for my mother, some memory still remains, and she flexes it, like a phantom limb: "I'm sorry I don't have anything in the house to offer you," she says, as if there is still a pantry and a refrigerator and she is just low for the moment. Or, "I straightened up this morning." She *does* "straighten up," which means that she tries to wash her own soiled clothing, though she doesn't have the strength, or soap, or eyesight to do it properly.)

As for the larger sense of purpose—caring for a family, or mate, or having a job to go to, or something to accomplish—all this is gone, too. Can you imagine, if you didn't have to go to work, wash up, put the dishes in the dishwasher, pick up the mail, answer it, go to the cleaners, play golf, do a laundry, how much more time you would have to spend? How can they spend it all? What kind of life happens here?

This is the daily routine: They rise.

They dress or are dressed. No one in this facility remains in bedclothes all day. This is considered a positive value, or rather, it is a *bad* sign if the residents are in their bedclothes all day, or are poorly dressed, because it is a signal that the caretakers don't care. I read recently, in an article in the August 1995 *Consumer's Report* on how to shop for nursing homes that, "If residents are wearing soiled or ill-fitting clothes . . . or are inappropriately dressed for the season, don't put your relative among them. I read this, coincidentally, a day after I have visited my mother and found her wearing pink slacks under a red and green floral housecoat with a blue and purple floral polo shirt over the housecoat, and a soiled tan blazer topping off the outfit. She had on one beige sneaker and one white one. Believe me, if you had been visiting this place with an eye toward putting your parent here—and if the director did not succeed in steering you away from the sight of my mother first—you would definitely have assumed that she was ill-cared for. But, actually, it is a very caring and perceptive social worker who determines that it is more important for my mother to dress herself than for her to look good. So even though it is horrifying to see—I think of how my long-suffering mother must have viewed my flyaway hair and my penchant for purple all those years!—she still dresses herself.

Breakfast is served at seven o'clock.

After breakfast, around ten or so, there is usually a "program" held in the day room at the end of the hall. Sometimes it is arts and crafts, usually keyed to a specific holiday. On Five, where the level of cognition and attention span is low, they trace and cut out and color and sparkle-dust oaktag leaves for autumn, hearts for Valentine's Day, pumpkins for Halloween, and turkeys for Thanksgiving. They talk about the holidays and reminisce. Sometimes they have simple exercise geared, of course, to their level of ability and ability to follow instruction. In a circle, they lift hands and feet and put them down in rhythm. The beat is often disco music. Sometimes they play old-fashioned records, and sing along to old songs, "Let Me Call You Sweetheart," "Alexander's Ragtime Band." Sometimes they ballroom dance, taking turns being the partner of the rec therapist.

There is a "beauty parlor" once a week, and they are taken, by appointment, to another floor where they can get all the standard services: cut, wash, set, manicure.

The doctor and podiatrist come once a month, the optometrist every few months. Blood pressure is checked once a week, unless for specific complaints.

On other floors in this facility, the activities are larger in scope, and more ambitious and extensive. These are the ones my sister and I noted on the bulletin board in the lobby when we visited, and hoped to see my mother participating in: luncheons, discussion groups, religious services, trips to the racetrack and the mall, and musical shows. Occasionally, some of the higher functioning residents on Five are included in these. When my mother first came, she was among them; now she is rarely invited, and if she is, she refuses to go.

After morning activities, preparations for lunch begin. This means the dining room at the other end of the hall is open, and, at about half past eleven, the aides begin the big job of bringing them in to lunch—either by wheeling them in wheelchairs, or by lining them up, encouraging and reminding them and prodding them and walking them. This takes about half an hour. (My mother goes in on her own, most days, though she may not stay.) The dining room is kept closed except at mealtimes, and when it is opened a shrill alarm goes off. From about eleven o'clock on, the alarm keeps sounding, because residents are anxious to get their seats. (There is a quite common anxiety about whether they are entitled to a meal at each mealtime, and frequently my mother has to be reassured that she does not have to pay for her meal, that it is "all included.") Many residents of Five do not remember that they have just eaten, so they are often hungry. (When I come to visit, my mother always says, "I'm starved." I always bring food. They tell me not to bring snacks because they ruin her appetite, but I bring them anyway. At her age, if she wants to ruin her appetite and eat junk, why not?)

After lunch, there is some mid-afternoon activity. Sometimes there is a musical entertainer. Coffee is served at about half past three.

Throughout the day, many of the residents' doors remain open and televisions can be heard playing (though on Five most of the residents do not have the working memory to follow a program). You can see people lying on their beds, eyes open or closed, but not many. Residents are encouraged to come to the day room. Some participate in whatever activity is going on, others just sit.

Dinner is at 5:30 P.M.

That's about it.

Most life is lived within the walls of the Home, and mostly on that floor. In good weather, residents of Five are taken outside as a group. That is the only way you can go out from that floor, unless you have a visitor who takes you. There are two or three freelance companions in the home who, for a reasonable fee, will do a special task, such as accompany your relative outside, or take her to the beauty parlor and stay with her, or just spend an hour. (We tried this, but for a long time my mother refused to go with whomever we hired; none of them were good enough to fool her into thinking they wanted her company, which, I think, is what it would have taken for her to go along. She had enough critical judgment to decide she didn't care to spend time with a hired stranger. Lately, she allows herself to get taken. An improvement but a sad one. She no longer notices if someone is a stranger.)

Residents don't talk on the phone, they can't go out by themselves, they have no chores to do. What do they do? Beside the "programs" or sitting in the dayroom? They walk up and down the corridors if they have mobility, holding on to the rails that run the length from end to end. They sleep. They have visitors.

I wonder if it takes intense concentration to accomplish even the simple chores of walking straight down the hallway and finding your room, getting through a meal, and if this concentration makes time go by.

I have heard that the average stay in a nursing home is supposedly two years. I think on Five it must be longer, because many of these people are basically physically healthy; it is just their minds that are gone.

The people who have been there since my mother came are: A, a solid-looking Italian woman, to whom I was introduced when I first came to visit the place, and was shown this floor (and I remember her so well because her affect was warm and friendly and she seemed so much *there* that I did not register that this was the senile dementia floor). When my mother first came, A was definitely a meeter and a greeter. She had Brooklyn in her voice, and you imagined her being loved by the nieces and nephews and making a good

red gravy. She is now very much changed; she is petu-
lant, childlike, often angry. She has lost a lot of weight.
She doesn't know which room is hers anymore, and she
doesn't smile. She is often (or always, I am not sure) in a
wheelchair.

S is eerie. She is much younger looking than anyone
else on this floor. Her face is widely planed, unlined, and
shiny, so she almost looks like she has had facial surgery,
dermabrasion. She has only one expression, a slight smile.
Her hair is blondish white and straight; it is cut bluntly
and hangs almost fashionably to just above her shoulders.
She speaks in German and possibly in tongues. I do not
believe she speaks English. She wanders, often into other
people's rooms. Lately, she has begun to look older and
has begun to carry a stuffed animal around with her. At
the beginning, I called her the ax murderer, because her
youthfulness and flat demeanor is mysterious and scary,
like something out of a B movie. She doesn't scare me
anymore. Still, hers is the story I am most curious about,
but the nurses don't tell any tales.

M, my mother's next-door neighbor, is very normal-
looking. (What is it that signals you that someone is not
"normal" just by looking at her? Two different shoes?
Uncombed hair, a wild-eyed expression or a vacant-
eyed one? Clothing that doesn't fit? Doesn't match?
Layers of clothes on top of each other, like a dress over
slacks?) M is always well dressed, neat and clean. Her

daughter does her laundry. She addresses everyone the same way whether she knows them or not: "Hello, mameleh," "Goodbye, mameleh." She is recently in a wheelchair, unable to walk, but with nothing organically wrong. Her daughter says the last time she went to the hospital she was in bed for about two weeks, and in that time, forgot how to walk.

A man paces endlessly, up and down the hallways, crying "help me, help me." At mealtimes he is assigned to my mother's table, but table-hops, eating butter off the plates. He reminds my sister of the Arte Johnson character on Laugh-In, and he does have that gravelly voice in which, one day, he says to my sister, confidentially and suggestively, "You got any time for me?"

R, the roly-poly woman, is a former opera singer. She is always complimentary of your appearance and tries not to let you get by without a greeting. "Hello, beeyootiful," she says. "How are you today, beeyootiful?"

There is another former singer, "from the show business." She is tough and seems jovial but you never know when she is going to think the joke is on her and get mad. She is now in a wheelchair, but when we first came, she was very peppy.

There is L, a friendly lady whose face is peeling and raw with some type of eczema; her roommate is a mannish woman who always wears a baseball hat and never speaks and clings to the friendly lady. The friendly lady always has a smile. My mother calls the roommate her "husband."

M and G are the only husband and wife on Five. They are both in wheelchairs. He doesn't say anything. She is always screaming for him, where is he, how is she going to find him, and when she finds him, she screams where were you? (I have just heard that he died. I wonder if she will know this, or forever after think he is lost and keep calling him.)

There is a woman with a brogue who asks over and over and over if you will take her home. She lived in the Bronx. Lately, she is, strapped into a wheelchair.

Y talks to an imaginary friend. The conversations are about fresh fish, black pocketbooks, buying a pound of plums, picking up newspapers, arguing over what someone said. Her friend has a name and she repeats it often in a husky ex-cigarette smoker's voice in the course of the conversations, which she has as she walks up and down the long corridor on her walker. You think this is crazy? I don't find this crazy. Her friend's presence brings her obvious pleasure, and the daily life that she reviews in these conversations sounds like a good one. She does not seem to notice the world around her. This is how she lives on Five.

What about my mother? How much of Five does she take in? What is it like for her? What kind of adjustment does she make? What choices?

At certain times she seems to think she is still living in an apartment building. She picks and chooses among her "neighbors" and ignores a lot of the craziness that goes on around her. For instance, she filters out the bloodcurdling screams for help that sometimes fill the corridor. (These are as much cries of existential pain as from proximate causes. You get to know the difference.) If I say to her, "Wow, someone's yelling," she says, "Oh, pay no attention," and calls me back to what we were talking about. I think about how all her life she taught us and believed herself in the absolute value of "mind your own business" and "don't get involved." She isn't curious, she isn't sympathetic, and she doesn't wonder if she can be of some assistance. When I was a kid and someone had hurt my feelings or something made me feel bad, she used to say, "Don't you care!" to which I used to scream in frustration, "But I do!" Here it serves her well. She *wills* herself not to see and not to care for her own good.

Some of what goes on she views as bad behavior and disapproves of, though she doesn't see it as bizarre or crazy. The lady with the brogue, for instance, begging to go home is "always bellyaching" according to my mother. To me, the repetitious nature of the lady's chanting is a kind of desperate grasp of one last reality. But to my mother, who never had any patience for people who complain out loud, especially to strangers, it is low class. It lacks breeding. She has always looked down on people who "go to the extreme" and so she steers clear of "mameleh," presumably because of the indiscriminate use of an endearment, and of R, who sometimes bursts into loud song.

She leans heavily on her identity as a teacher. It still makes her proud. Everyone knows she is a teacher.

"I have to get a job," she says to me. "I can't sit around here and do nothing."

Sometimes she's back at school. A bell rings to call a nurse: It's the end of a period or the beginning of assembly. A loudspeaker calls someone to the fifth floor desk: It's the principal summoning someone to the main office. When she leaves the Home, whether it is to be taken to the emergency room of the local hospital, or out to lunch, she has the distinct feeling she has left her classroom, and she is always anxious to get back to it. "They took me right out of my classroom," she says or "Who dismissed my class?" and when they are taken out as a group, she says, "I came down with my class."

Sometimes, the recreation therapist uses this fantasy to coax my mother into activities. "Mary," she'll say, "we're doing paperwork in the office, and we need you." She means coloring and cutouts in the dayroom. My mother's eyes light up. "Paperwork" is a school word. Sometimes she is content to do paperwork as a favored pupil or class monitor. She respects the rules and she likes being able to follow instructions. But occasionally this fantasy is also a source of confusion and anxiety for her. At times like this, the delusion that she is in school is so strong that she worries about going "home." Sometimes she can be distracted out of it, and sometimes she can't. She is convinced she has come to the "school" in the morning and she does not know how she will get home. I am reminded of a teacher friend of hers who once got locked into the school right across the street from where we lived, after hours, and I remember this lady standing behind the locked gates, screaming for someone to release her. I wonder if somewhere in the recesses of her mind, my mother remembers this, too. I wonder if it's a common old teacher nightmare. She no longer likes to go outside. She feels they will close up her school, dismiss her class, and she will be lost.

Recently, on a summer afternoon, I brought a picnic lunch. She lasts about ten minutes before she starts talking about who is covering her class. I remind her that the nurse has told her it is okay to go out and have a good time. But she can't stop.

"Oh, I'm so sorry to give you so much trouble. But who is going to take me home?"

"You live here, mom."

"No, I *don't*."

"Believe me, you do."

"Bette, I can't *live* here. I come here in the morning. I came here this morning. I go *home*."

"This is your home."

"No, no it isn't, don't tell me this, it can't be, I have a home . . ."

"Mom, this is a nursing home."

But she seems not to hear me. "What about furniture? What about all my things?"

"Mom, this is a nursing home. We gave up your apartment almost three years ago, and you *have* been living here."

"Don't tell me. I know. Where do I sleep? I don't sleep here?"

"Yes, you do. You have a bed."

"Show me."

"OK."

"Take me, stay with me, show me."

"I will. But first let's finish lunch."

And so, three years late, we have the conversation I had dreaded the first day that we brought her here. Had she dreaded it, too? Have we both delayed it subconsciously until it is almost bearable? Three years delayed it is just almost bearable. I distract her for a few minutes, with sliced pickle, with other talk, but she comes back to it. "You live here," I say.

"I know I do. Why don't I remember?" Yet, as soon as we hit the fifth floor and step off the elevator, she knows where she is. "This way," she says, and leads me to her room.

It is common for residents on Five to wander into other residents' rooms. They don't always know which room is theirs. My mother still knows it, at this writing, though I notice lately that on a bad day she is tenuous about identifying it—double-checks name, number on the door, name again, and occasionally a hesitant "This is not my room, is it?"

On the other hand, she doesn't cut any slack for anyone else's confusion. Because her room is close to the dining room, it is popular with wanderers who had been on their way to lunch and then maybe forgot halfway and think they were heading home to lie down, or in the midst of the trip need a bathroom. Once, my mother came in and found S in her room, and she has not forgotten it since, nor will she forgive her. (It astonishes me how tenacious that bit of memory is, while so much else is like writing on water.) If I smile at S she tells me not to, and repeats the story. There are several colorful variations on it, but most of them involve a dog. (S carries a stuffed animal. In my mother's story it is a real one.) Another time, she finds the man who ate butter in her bed.

"What did you do?" I say.

"I told him to get the hell out," she says.

Once, when my daughter is visiting, my mother and

a woman who wanders in and refuses to leave almost come to blows. As my daughter tells it: The woman enters, flattens herself against the door and screams for my mother and my daughter to get out of *her* room. My mother says, "She's crazy," and tries to go on talking. But this woman will have none of it. My daughter tries to explain to her that she is mistaken but she just keeps screaming "Get out, get out, get out." And then my mother gets insulted and calls her a punk (!) and starts advancing on her, winding up and threatening to "give her my tennis hand." My daughter is panicky, by this time. She's afraid to pull them apart, for fear she'll hurt someone, and the woman is blocking the door, and my mother is getting ready to whack her one. Finally, she manages to get the door open and edge the woman into the open doorway. But my mother tries to squash the woman between the door and the frame. My daughter yells for help, and an aide comes and calmly leads the woman, who is suddenly perfectly docile, away. My daughter is shaken by the absolutely irrational and antisocial behavior, and by her own inability to stop it. I giggle when she tells the story, partially because she tells it on herself, with her, cowering there, while these two small ninety-year-olds square off. But I'm also laughing because, being super-civilized myself, there's something bracing about the prospect of not caring anymore. The problem is, by the time I'm so

old I don't care, I won't know I don't care and it won't
feel bracing, it will just be the only way I know to do
it. We try telling my mother the intruders don't mean
any harm, they are just a little mixed up, but she can't
understand what we are talking about, and she doesn't
want to hear it. Anyway, it is not quite as big a stretch
for my mother as all that. She was always selective about
whom she invited into her home. Lately, she doesn't
even want the housekeeping or nursing staff to come
in. Her sense of privacy is unchanged, but her mind has
not registered the change of situation which makes this
kind of privacy no longer possible for her.

Some of the bizarre things that go on around my
mother seem perfectly natural to her.

For example, on one of our early visits, she points to
the ex-showbiz singer. "See that woman?" she says. We
are sitting in the dayroom, and the afternoon sun is
warming our strip of seats along the western wall of the
room.

"Yes," I say, supressing an urge to tell her not to point.

"Well, she owns that wall," she says, pointing now at
the wall opposite us.

"Ma?" I say.

She acknowledges my disbelief, but doesn't seem to
see anything unusual. "Listen, I don't know," she says,
"Her husband was a very rich man and he bought her
that wall. That's what she says." (This is a very common

phrase, coming from my mother. We hear it often. It is the way life worked for her, or the way she thought it worked. "Her son owns . . . her husband owned . . ." explains all sorts of excellent conditions and high rank.)

The next time I come, the woman owns the seats that take the afternoon sun, but she lets us sit there anyway. Shortly afterward, we are told that this lady rescinded her permission when my mother wanted to sit down, and my mother refused to sit at that end of the room for a while, even if the lady wasn't there.

I wonder if the reason my mother accepts the bizarre statements of other people is because her own life now includes such occurrences as the arrival and disappearance of my father, of my grandparents, of men on telephone wires, and other hallucinations. I wonder if this adds variety to her life. It does not seem to frighten her. At least not so far.

Months later, my mother confesses to my sister that the lady who owned that wall taught her how to steal, but she doesn't do it anymore.

"What did you take?" my sister says.

"Socks," my mother says.

Interesting, I don't doubt this. As with the incident in which she was ready to defend herself with her hands, I can see my mother's uncorked desire to *have* leading to her feeling justified in *taking*. Maybe this also explains the picture we find in the top drawer of my mother's bureau, of a man who looks vaguely like my father, but turns out to be the man across the hall. We don't mention it, and eventually it disappears.

Ownership, as a concept, is alive on Five, though it is a little cockeyed. When my mother came, she brought with her, or rather Kate brought for her, some of her favorite knicknacks—a china figurine, a flowered bud vase, a small needlepoint. Within weeks, they were gone. We reported it, of course, but they never turned up. Barring the possibility that there is a ring of resident-thieves working the fifth floor, here's what I imagine happens: Knicknacks and doodads that were popular in everyone's household fifty and sixty years ago, Spode teacups, those light green soapstone ashtrays everybody's mother had, family pictures with indistinct families in front of a tree or at the seashore get passed around from room to room. Someone will wander into someone else's room. She will see that Hummel kissin' boy and girl that used to sit on her dresser, and she will think, "Oh, *there* it is," and she will pick it up, maybe to dust it, but just in the middle of this action, she will remember she was on her way out the door to go to . . . and then, in the middle of *that* action, maybe, she will find herself back in her own room, with her Hummel kissin' boy and girl in her hand, and thinking she just picked it up and dusted it, she will put it back on her dresser. I have no doubt that the picture of the old man that my mother had is in someone else's drawer now. (The man himself is gone.) When your eyesight and your memory are a little spotty, who can tell the difference between yours and mine, hers and hers?

Residents' clothing is labeled, and dirty laundry is collected from each resident and brought to the in-house laundry, but when it is returned, wrapped in plastic with the resident's name and room number on it, pieces are often missing, or other residents' clothing is mixed in. My mother's clothes disappear routinely, and I find things that belong to other people in her closet. We tried to straighten it out, but it seems impossible. My mother does not notice.

Sometimes, when Five seems neither my mother's old home or her old school, when she is at her lowest, it seems Five is a hospital to her. "What am I doing here?" she says, then. "I'm not sick."

## On Friendship and Sociability

BEING central to someone else's life, someone's "one and only" makes you feel important and gives a sense of belonging that nothing else does. Being irreplaceable to even one single other person—so your name appears on some dotted line where it says, "In Case Of Emergency Please Notify" or someone expects and needs your presence on a daily basis—is a great source of strength. When this kind of relationship goes, I don't think you ever quite recover the same sense of power that being the linchpin in a family or the head of a department at work gives you. Empty nest, widowhood, retirement. They are defining experiences of late middle age, and when they occur, we instinctively struggle to shift our positions. By reestablishing the kind of "you're the one" relationships with spouses we may have started out with (or we can't, and the marriage crumbles), we find ourselves making our way back to families, if we have them, to old friends. As long as we have the ability, we seek that sense of centrality, because without it we have to worry about every Thanksgiving. Without it, we're off the map. A lot of old people, especially those in nursing homes, are off the map.

After my father died, I watched my mother survive this loss of centrality and reestablish it over and over again. Friendship, to her, was a pragmatic affair: Her friends were the people she worked with or lived near, who had common interests or liked to play cards or mah-jongg. They had to be, in her assessment, refined, intelligent, and not prone to gossip. Her friends had something to offer her, and she offered them the honor of her attention. People were drawn to her, I think, because of her independence as well as her charm. Her friends felt "chosen."

But what is it like now? What form does friendship take on Five? What can a friend with senile dementia offer? What can a friend with senile dementia want?

Though there are people on Five who lack affect, and some who are animated only and completely within their own worlds (like Y), there are others who still crave the give-and-take of human contact, and continue to give and take it against all odds. They trade the last shreds and shards of social vocabulary—Hello mamaleh, how are you, fine, you look nice, my children are coming, what time is lunch? It's a beautiful day, what's that smell?—like working capital. My mother is one of those.

In her first months on Five, she and L, the little lady with the eczema on her face, both imagine that they grew up together in the Bronx. This is not true. I don't know which of them thought of it first, or how they keep it going, but it is the basis for stopping in the corridor, on the back-and-forth strolls that take up their time, for a friendly chat. The chat may not make all that much sense, but the tone is warm and friendly. (And which of us hasn't experienced those kinds of relationships?)

My mother says, "This is my daughter." And to me, "This is L. We have known each other for years."

L smiles at me and says to my mother, "He's very nice, very handsome."

My mother seems to ignore the gender-bender. (Is this out of politeness, or doesn't she notice?) "She came to visit," she says.

"What can I tell you," the woman says. "Some days good, some days bad."

"That's all right," my mother says, taking the sharp conversation turn on two wheels. "I think we missed lunch."

My mother and this lady are no longer friends. Maybe it is one of those friendships that just didn't get off the ground. Or maybe the roommate scared my mother off. This woman and her roommate, the one who wears a baseball cap and whom my mother always refers to as her "husband," are very exclusive to each other. One day, the roommate approached us as we were walking in the hall, and hit my mother's arm. I stepped between them and said, "No!" My mother acted like she didn't even notice it. But maybe she understood the relationship to be like a marriage, and she didn't want to come between them.

My mother also converses with members of the staff, the nurses, the recreation therapists, the social worker, and lately with a psychotherapist who has been assigned to her. She attempts to put her "best foot forward" whenever possible. "This beautiful young lady has been helping me," she might say, if I walk in and find an aide trying to get her to come for a bath. She raises her eyebrows at me to let me know she doesn't mean it. "Thank you, dear," she says, as the aide leaves. She retains the cues and openers to our particular and familiar conversations, even on days when she may not know exactly who we are: How are the children? How is your job? What do you do? How is . . . your husband? (Carefully, tactfully, so I don't know she has forgotten Marvin's name.) She talks about teaching, and about life, and about tennis. (She thinks the psychotherapist is a tennis pro. She tells my sister that some man comes down the fire escape from another floor in the building and comes into her room through the window to talk to her about tennis. She enjoys the talk.)

The recreational activities and mealtimes are important occasions for human contact, with lots of direction and encouragement from the aides, the nursing staff, and the recreational therapists. Seating at meals is crucial, since this is the last remaining social ritual, and whom you sit with at meals is, in a sense, whom you are related to. At first, my mother is seated unhappily. (The man who ate butter was one of her tablemates.) Then for a while, she sits with the man and wife and a fourth person. That is okay, she never complains, but she thinks the man is paying for her meals (since, in her day, when you were dining out it was the man's "treat") and it becomes a constant worry for her that the wife might not like it. (Does that mean that she did? Did she feel like a femme fatale? ) Now she is at a table with H and A, who have become her friends. A has a nice, colloquial style and is very forthcoming. If you ask her how she is, she says, cheerfully, "Oh, okay, draggin' along," and she looks down at her walker. Her style is so appealing that it takes several sentences to notice she is not making sense. Once, I took A downstairs with my mother and me, to sit in the lobby. But my mother gets very annoyed when I pay attention to anyone else, and A is talkative. (Or is she annoyed because she still can't stand people who talk too much?) I spent the whole time watching my mother's impatience, hoping she wouldn't tell A to shut up.

H is my mother's special friend, her one and only. H is tall and thin and dignified looking. When she first arrived, she dressed in suits and stockings and heels. Now she is in an unmatched outfit, her hair in tangles, but she still carries a handbag. Carrying a handbag is an important last connection to the world outside. My mother still carries hers. Inside are old envelopes, sometimes a note (in an increasingly illegible hand) to me or my sister complaining that we do not visit, once a pint container of milk, occasionally toast. But she won't leave her room without it, and still says, "Where's my bag?" as I remember her saying all the years I have known her, whenever she left home. My mother and H go to recreation together, visit one another in their rooms, and call for each other to go to meals. They "hang together," as one of the nurses says. Like my mother, H was a working woman once, a model. H believes she and my mother know each other from long ago. She also thinks my sister is a member of her family. Part of the Philadelphia branch.

When I walk my mother into lunch one day, and say hello to H the usual question follows: "How do you know H?"

"From you," I tell my mother.

H, who has acknowledged my greeting with pleasure, then says to me, "You know her?" indicating my mother.

"She's my mother," I say.

"I'm in shock!" H says. "I've lived on the same block with her for years and years and years and I didn't know. I'm in shock!"

This is pleasant shock. This is social shock. Presumably, she knew me and didn't know I knew my mother and she knew my mother and didn't know my mother was related to me.

Meanwhile, my mother is asking me again how I know H, and I don't want her to feel ignored while I am talking to H, so I try to answer her and carry on the conversation with H at the same time.

"What is she talking about?" my mother is saying. "When are you coming back? Why can't you stay for lunch?"

"I'm in shock!" H is saying again. "I have known her such a long time and I didn't know you were her mother." ( She says this to me.)

I am swiveling back and forth between them. "Well I am." "Soon." "No, I mean I'm her daughter." "Because I have to go to work."

"You're her daughter?" she says to my mother. "I'm in shock!"

I leave them there, companionable in their certainty of a shared past.

I think what my mother offers and wants as a friend now is a sense that she chooses and is chosen by someone of superior qualities (somewhat like herself, a loner, a professional woman, *fine*), that she has someone to walk and talk with, and that person and she have a regular life together. It seems remarkably similar to the way it always was.

THE dayroom is bright and its windows look out onto the ocean. At one end is a long table. This is where the residents do their crafts and sometimes pass a medicine ball from one to the other. When they do, the therapist makes sure to personalize the activity. "Mary got it, now she passed it to H, now H has it, come on H, give A a chance . . ."

There are two recreational therapists, and sometimes they have an assistant. G is tall and very pretty, and quite bubbly. P is slight and younger and her style is much more subdued. Both of them are loving and kind to the residents of Five. It seems to me that there are three things they offer which are crucial to my mother's quality of life: the pleasure of busy hands (arts and crafts), the power of music, and the importance of personal contact. Both therapists seem to take a real joy in the music, and they use touch to cue the residents in games and responses and out of affection. Sometimes it seems to make them happy. Sometimes it doesn't.

On a typical weekday morning, when I come to visit, I find my mother in the dayroom. She is sitting in a circle of women, many in wheelchairs, and G is in the center of the circle. They are about to do exercises. Music is playing. I stop in the doorway, and she spots me immediately. Her eyes light up.

G says, "Oh, Mary, here's your daughter." (G seems to know people's relatives.) G is bopping to the music and so I come bopping across the circle to my mother, to make my mother laugh. She does, and preens and kisses me. I go to find a seat, but she interrupts G, telling her to "get a chair for my daughter" and G brings me a chair. (I enjoy my mother's slightly imperious tone, because it is so much like the old Mary. G seems to enjoy it too, as if anyone in my mother's position who can still use that tone is *something*.) I sit in the circle opposite my mother and join in. She is animated and excited, and she and I make eye contact, and at opposite ends of the circle, we exercise together. The movements are gently stretching ones. Some of the residents follow G, some of them don't, some of them do sporadically. She does not make a fuss, though she does try, gently, to push the envelope.

"Now we are going to wash the windows," she says, for big arm movements. I see a quizzical look come over my mother's face, as if to say, "Who wants to do that?" And when G says, "We are going to mop the floor now" for a forward push of the arms, my mother gets the look again, and G catches it and says, "Oh, no, Mary doesn't want to do that," and my mother blushes and laughs. I think, oh, the elitist, she's still at it.

Then G puts on some dance music. It is time to dance. Mother calls out to her, "Get my daughter up there dancing," and I say, "I will if you will, mom. Come on," but she says no. I get up and go over to her and try to coax her up to dance with me, and she whispers, "No, I'll be very embarrassed. Now give me a kiss and go back and sit down." Just as if I am a little girl again and am "acting up." Yet I can see she is very proud that I am there. G dances with the woman who wears the baseball hat. This old woman is an outstanding dancer, she twirls and bends fluidly and really "gets into" the music. G beams. The woman wants to dance close, romantically, and G gently extricates herself from the embrace. Then G dances with S, who also seems to get joy out of movement. Her face, usually frozen, is relaxed and pink with pleasure. The group is in good spirits, high spirits, and there is a buzz and a low level of pleasure among them. Then G orients them. This is what she says. "I want to let you know . . ." she turns from one part of the circle to the other, repeating, for the deaf ears among them, ". . . I want to let you know that this place that you are in is a nursing home. It is a very safe place for you to be. They do your laundry here, and clean your room, and even clean *you*, whether you like it or not!" My mother frowns slightly at that. "And today is . . ."

I mouth the answer at my mother, and she calls out, "Monday!"

"Good, Mary," G says, and we are in the classroom again, this time my mother is the prize pupil and G is the teacher. "And the month is . . ."

My mother hardly looks at me for confirmation before shouting "October!"

"Right, Mary!" G says. "It is the month of October. And today's date is the . . ." and she points to the big calendar on the wall and my mother says, "Twenty-fourth. My daughter told me. Bette told me." She is an honorable pupil and can't take credit for another pupil's smarts.

"That's right," G says. "And if you forget what day it

is, you just look at the wall over there and you can find out. And now we are going to go in and get ready for lunch. But ladies, don't go and get into your nightgowns after lunch, don't climb into bed . . . hear that, Mary? Hear that H . . . ?" Because my mother sometimes finishes up the day right after lunch, thinking it's nighttime and the meal she's had is dinner. "Because we are going to go to a big musical show after lunch."

There is more than one way to look at this scene. I'm not Pollyanna, and I'd have to be blind not to see the obvious: here are mothers and grandmothers. Here are represented maybe a hundred years of accumulated abilities and accomplishments—pies crimpled like no one else could crimp them, children reared, tragedies borne, classes taught, arias sung, dances danced—plowed under, gone. This is one way for me to see it. I am witness to the downfall of the mighty. But, and this is a big BUT—the fallen don't see it this way. This is not what my mother sees, or feels. She can't, anymore. And I can't require her to see or feel or behave as I do (anymore than I require it of my grown children). I have to tune in to what she is feeling, what this moment does for her. This is a joyful moment in her life. She is, to the best of her remaining ability, participating in her life, asserting what self she has left, and feeling wonderful— warmed by the activity and by having me there to witness and share it with her. In some ways, this is an enrichment, a moment that has a value over and above when and where it is taking place, because my then-mother would never have permitted such a loving public exchange when she was younger.

But another day, it doesn't go so well. P is doing nursery rhymes. She starts one and they have to finish it. Then they kick a large inflated beach ball around a circle. She instructs them to aim low, and use their feet, and when some punch it or kick it high, she scolds cheerfully, and reiterates her instructions. But their attention seems ragged today. A few more people come into the circle. Another daughter brings her mother, and we squeeze her in, moving the chairs around. (Residents' families are always welcome here.) Two aides bring two other women. One of them is complaining that she is missing her ring. P ignores this, as she has ignored a woman in a wheelchair who has been saying, "I have to go to the bathroom" for about ten minutes. I assume, since the woman's cries do not get more urgent, that P knows what she is ignoring. Maybe the woman is feeling the impulse but P knows better—that she is wearing a diaper, perhaps, and it just doesn't matter if she wets or not. The other woman who sits down begins to complain very loudly, like this: "I am warning you, there is a very bad man, and he is going to kill all my children, and he is going to kill all of us, and if you don't watch out, he is going to kill you. I am not going to play a game now, my heart is hurting, if only you knew what that man did to me, he is going to kill everyone." Many of the residents, and P, don't seem to notice what she is saying. But one woman says, irritably, "What is she talking about?" Another one, quite with-it, like my mother was at the beginning, looks upset. And when the woman repeats that her heart is hurting and the man is going to kill all of us, and no one knows the terrible things he has done or else they wouldn't be playing games, she suddenly bursts out, "Keep quiet and stop talking about death. What's the matter with you? You don't talk about death!" The woman who lost her ring starts saying "I am going to call the police." I have a sense that P is losing them. She gets a large, light sheet made of parachute material in rays of blue, yellow, red, and white with a hole in the center and handles around the edge, and she goes around giving a handle to each woman in the circle, and they are to toss the ball till it hits the ceiling. It is excellent exercise, and the woman who lost her ring joins in; but the other one keeps talking about the bad man who is going to kill us all.

AFTER a good recreational session, my mother is jazzed up. The music and the activity have jazzed her up. She walks back to her room energetically. She and I walk in rhythm to the last song, and we sing it together. There is half an hour before lunch and I will stay with her until then. I brought her a new pair of slacks and she has the energy to try them on so I can measure the hem. I pin them, and then she puts on an old pair while I hem the new ones.

She wonders where my father is. I tell her he is long gone.

"He is?"

"Sure, don't you remember?" I say.

"What did he die of?"

"His heart. He was a great guy, wasn't he?" I say.

She smiles. "He sure was. He read a lot and he was a tennis player and he wrote stories."

"He had a lot of life to him, didn't he?" I say.

"He sure did," she says.

"You think he's in heaven?" I say.

She laughs. "Oh, no, not your father."

"He had a sense of humor, too," I say.

"Oh, yes he did," she says. Then she takes conversational initiative. "Was he a good father?"

I try not to patronize my mother, so I say the truth. I say, "Well, I don't think so. I think he raised us with values, though." I have just heard my sister say this. It is the kind of thing my mother might have said. But now she just looks puzzled. "Value? What do you mean by that?" She doesn't understand the word. Or, it does not have the abstract sense any more in her mind. I try to explain, and she is not discomfited that she does not know. She doesn't *know* anymore that she is supposed to know this thing.

She kisses me. She says, "Well, I'm very much alone, here. You kids have your jobs, your kids, your lives. I can't hang around here all alone. I have to get a job, do something." This is a common conversational thread. Sometimes I tell her that the school system is lousy nowadays, with metal detectors so the kids can't bring weapons into the school. Sometimes I say they are laying off teachers and there are no openings. She likes this, it's school system gossip. Today I stick closer to the truth; I think because she is so sharp, I want to merge our worlds. So I say she is retired, and they wouldn't hire her back, so why not just enjoy retirement?

"But mentally, do you think I could do it? Am I up to it?" she says.

"Mentally, sure, but your memory is shot," I say. It is my limited ability to lie that makes me put a little truth in it.

"Really?" she says.

"It isn't your fault," I say. "It's the process of aging. Hardening of the arteries."

"But if I read, and talk to people, doesn't that help?" she says.

"Of course it does," I say, and am both amazed at her cognitive strength on this, and feel a ghost of guilt at the fact that she is here, on Five, among people less able to reason and talk than she. (How do I know? Maybe they too, when stimulated by music, and warmth, and the sight and sound of their loved ones, make these leaps.) Then I remember that she does not now, even as I am thinking this, remember what she has just said, and that she cannot read, though she thinks she has just read.

Nevertheless, as I walk her in to lunch, I am promising myself I will double my visits, and contact the social worker and try to have her taken to other floors for more stimulating discussions and activities. But when my sister and I try and follow through on this, my mother refuses to go.

## Power and Who Wields It and How

IT is no secret that in American society, old age itself is a pretty profound state of powerlessness. Despite lip service about the wisdom and experience the older population brings, most people don't have much patience or respect for what old people have to say or what they can teach us. They're slow. We're getting faster and faster. In most workplaces (except maybe the U.S. Senate, which seems to have a soft spot for the senior, and occasionally the senile) the bias is toward youth. Still, as long as an old person can impersonate a middle-aged one, cosmetically or otherwise, or maintain a vigor roughly equal, or superior to, what everyone expects, the old person can find a grudging respect. "How old did you say she is?" "Well, God bless 'er, look at her go!" The tone is a mixture of amusement, faint disbelief and condescension, and implies superiority. It says, "I have the power to bestow a blessing on this adult person who didn't even ask me for one, and I'm not even clergy."

In a nursing home, the subtle power to condescend is the least of it.

In a nursing home, *everyone* has power over the old, especially the old who are physically or mentally impaired. From the top down, director, doctor, nurses, support staff (physical therapy, social work, recreational therapy), aides all have something to say about how the life of this elderly resident will be conducted. A "care plan" is drawn up and decided upon by all these powerful people, though the resident herself does not attend the congress at which its articles are drawn. (The family of the resident is consulted, so you can add them to the list of the powerful.) Well, of course, if a resident has senile dementia, how can she be expected to participate in her own care? There's nothing wrong, in itself, with getting together and planning a way to make life easy for an old person. But the very fact that it is done without the resident's own approval suggests the enormous delicacy with which these decision-makers have to wield their power in order not to abuse it. It also suggests that if you have a relative in a nursing home, you have to keep watch all the time.

Patronization is a fairly benign use/abuse of power, but it colors almost every social interraction a resident is likely to have. You hear it in that kindergarten-teacher, manic-cheerful voice, in the pronoun we (as in "How are we, today, Mary?"). It is common to hear one of the aides or a therapist or nurse call an elderly patient by an endearment usually reserved for close relations, or children: "Honey" or "Sweetie." It is what my mother's generation would have called "taking liberties." I have heard a recreational therapist say, of my mother, "She's so cute," or "Yer a good kid, Mary." If I called her on it, she might not even have noticed what she was saying, and surely she would say she doesn't mean anything bad by it. Surely she doesn't, and I don't call her on it. But when I hear it, and I hear it often, it seems to me that speaker subscribes to the belief that extreme age is a "second childhood" so it is all right to speak to old people as if they were children again.

But of course, despite the fact that some behaviors of old age mimic children's behaviors—in regard to toileting, perhaps, or tempers—old people are not children in important and obvious ways. Children are in the process of acquiring knowledge, while old people are in the process of divesting knowledge, involuntarily. And this loss of knowledge is complicated by the fact that old

people have long histories (partly or wholly remembered) and aptitudes that, though ghostly, may still
remain. My mother traces the trajectory of a good back-
swing, and I see in the way she holds her hand that she
remembers her grip. (I will bring a racket for her to
hold; she will forget saying she wanted to play tennis
once more.)

I think of children. How benevolently amused we
are when they sometimes exaggerate their own skills.
A kid says, "I'm a big girl, I can run faster than the
wind," and you answer, "You can, can you?" The skepti-
cal amusement is not an indictment and it isn't harsh. At
best, it's a challenge and can be overturned when the
youngster wins the race. But when my mother says, "I
can still play ball," she is talking about an aptitude she
once had in abundance, and hasn't the cognition to
realize is gone, but has just enough memory to long for.
Then, "You can, can you?" turns mean. The jovial skep-
tic is carelessly cruel, wielding a superior knowledge.
Because she knows my mother is never going to win
another game.

I walk around wanting to correct and direct everyone's response. I would like people to nudge the conversation toward reality, without comprising dignity. When
she says, "I can still play ball," next time, I want you to
say, "You were good, too!" instead of being amused at
her confusion and saying, "You can, can you?" or "God

bless 'er." Of course, I don't go around correcting every-one, because most of the people who talk to her this way do it unconsciously, mean well, and aren't going to change. (I also want to reserve my complaints for more important things.)

Ironically, she does not seem as bothered by it as she once might have been. In her supremely pragmatic way, I imagine she takes it as my car battery might take it if it were low, drawing all essential energy toward its own survival, and away from the minor operations, the ciga-rette lighter, the radio, these occasional assaults on her dignity.

Most powerful of all the powerful people in the nursing home are the aides, the ones who are in inti-mate contact with the residents on a daily basis. They are the ones in charge of everything that matters: toilet-ing, diapering, washing, feeding. Their jobs, menial and most difficult, are also among the lowest paid. Where my mother lives, most of these aides are immigrant and minority women. The general population of the resi-dents is comprised of white, middle-class women, many of whom were in positions of power in relation to these aides when they were young, able to hire them and fire them, snub them or bar their entrance to schools. So you could say the potential for conflict and the abuse of power is strong. In my mother's facility, I have not seen any abusive behavior by the aides. My mother's aides—

they rotate, which is essential to them, I am told, to prevent burnout, but is not ideal from my point of view, because just as my mother gets used to one aide another one is assigned—seem, for the most part, even-tempered and pleasant. However, as I write this, there is a power struggle going on, involving my mother and her aides. Each aide wants "her" residents to look good, be clean and well-dressed, because it represents (to the aide, I would assume, as well as to her superiors on the job) doing a good job. But my mother wants to dress herself and bathe herself. She is fighting to retain power over her own body. And she perceives (I think, correctly) that this is not a minor concession, were she to make it. Her entire life has come down to this. But she has forgotten how to do these things adequately, or forgets to do them at all.

"Oh, she gave me so much trouble this morning!" an aide tells me. She goes on to say that my mother had put on too many clothes, two different shoes, and the aide doesn't want one of "hers" going into the dining room like that, so she brings my mother back into her room and tries to get her to take some of the clothes off, but my mother fights her, scratches her, and the aide has to leave the room.

She tells me this cheerfully, and my mother says, "I'm sorry" to her when she hears it, and though I'm not sure she remembers what she did, she certainly does not seem inclined to refute it. The phrase which I latch on to and which concerns me is "tried to get her to . . ." And I wonder how this aide "brought" her into her room. Did she drag her? Did she pull her? Did she embarrass her? Did she dupe her? Did she speak sharply and intimidate her? I have never known how to get my mother to do something she didn't want to do. I wonder how this woman did. And once there, how did she "try" to get her undressed? Did she coax? Did she attempt to do it for her? I picture, hazily, a scenario in which my mother, civilization stripped from her by senility or powerlessness, lashes out.

The person whose job it is to collect laundry encounters my mother, fiercely protective of her dirty clothes and sheets, which she stashes in the wardrobe, under the bed, in drawers, in the bathtub. She refuses to give up her belongings and the laundry person must come back and confiscate the dirty wash when my mother isn't there. I know how hard this must make the aides' jobs. It must mess up their schedules to have to come back and get her laundry, or for another "try" at showering her, when she refuses the first time around. Hell, I know how stubborn she can be. But I want her to preserve her skills and her dignity because she wants to. And I don't want her forced. Yet it breaks my heart when I see what condition she is in—disorganized, messy, awful. The new social worker intervenes, telling the aides to let my mother dress herself, because it is more important than how she looks. I am grateful. Right, right, I say. I agree. But I can't help thinking how proud she used to be of how she looked. The social worker defers to me. She will have dressing mother included in the "care plan" if I and my sister wish it. So, the power is in our hands. I have to ask myself whether what breaks my heart the hour or so a week I see her matters, if it doesn't break hers. And I make the "right" decision, deferring to my mother's waning powers. And yet, whenever I take her out to lunch, I make sure to call ahead, and ask them to please have her ready for an outing. "Ready" is code for "dress her nicely" and "see that she is diapered" and I know it. So I wield my power, too.

Sometimes, condescension turns dark, and becomes real disrespect. There are people who assume that along with failing hearing and eyesight, old people's *selves* become dulled, and their feelings, and you don't have to care at all about what you say and do in front of them. Recently, after a visit to the dayroom, when I walk my mother back to her room, we find a member of the housekeeping staff mopping the floor. She is not cheerful at our interruption. "Don't come in, the floor is wet," she says.

"OK, we'll just wait out here till you're done, and then we'll tiptoe in."

"No," the woman snaps. "I just cleaned this."

My mother is tired, and it is a long walk back to the dayroom at the other end of the hall. The aide continues, "And she peepee in her bed every day and I got to clean that up, too!" She stares straight at my mother.

My mother doesn't get angry, but actually looks contrite, and denies it, saying, to me, "Bette, I don't, I swear I don't."

I am trembling inside. Very quietly, I ask this lady how she dares to speak this way about my mother. I tell her I will walk on her damn floor anytime I want. I say I hope that what has happened to my mother happens to her. Very soon. But instead of discharging my anger, this charges it, and by now I am shaking outwardly. My reaction is unexpected, to me, but I can't stop. I guess it has been building up. It is my mother who settles me down. She tells me not to care, to never mind. She says, "Come. Come away." She sees me close to making a scene, and she wants me to behave myself, and not make trouble. And senile though she is, she understands power. She understands that, though this aide has the most menial job in the nursing home, she feels perfectly comfortable venting her bad mood on this elderly resident. (The irony does not escape me: At this moment her "power" as a mother returns briefly, though she is not having a good or mentally organized day, as she tries to placate me.) This is the first and only time in three years that I have complained about someone in the home. The nurse sympathizes with me, and promises she will speak with the woman. The next time I see this worker, she is on another floor. I don't know whether this is a result of my complaint or the regular rotation of staff. I hope she does better with people on other floors.

By far, the worst abuse of power I have seen in connection with my mother has been in the emergency room of the hospital.

This past winter, my mother is taken there suffering from extreme abdominal pain. When I reach the hospital, some forty minutes later, I am told that I cannot see her because they are "working on her."

An hour and forty-five minutes later, I am allowed in. She lies, seemingly composed, in cubicle number six, small, quiet, chastened looking. She sees me and begins to cry. How did she get here? How did I know she was coming here? The confusion slowly reveals itself, and it is the old one. She thinks she has been brought here from "school." Everybody was all excited. One of her pupils' fathers drove her here. She knows it is a hospital. She knows she had a terrible pain. A moment later she forgets she had the pain. The pain seems to be gone. It seems that the ER doctors and nurses have not, in the two hours she has been here, "worked" on her at all. I fight to be rational. I know about triage, and she is not in extreme need. On the other hand, no one else seems to be, and nurses and doctors are standing around, chatting. I make an inquiry and am told "soon." They begin to "work" her up: EKG, blood, chest X ray. Another hour goes by.

A large, stocky male nurse says to me abruptly, "What is she on, Lasex? She's had to urinate about five times since she's been here." There is an unmistakeable impatience in his tone and I resist the urge to apologize for her. A second later, when she tells me she has to go to the bathroom, I think *"Uh oh."* I avoid the male nurse and approach a woman nurse. (Thinking, automatically, a woman will be more sympathetic.) She says she will come at once, but she doesn't. My mother begins to get anxious. Her old bladder can't wait. I see the nurse shuffling papers. I call her again, and she says, "oh," as if she has forgotten.

"Bedpan or bathroom?" she says. My mother says, timidly, "I would rather the bathroom?"

The nurse helps her sit up. My mother is frail and shaky, and needs help swinging her legs over the side of the bed. The bed is very high and my mother is very short. The nurse does not offer to roll it down, or maybe it isn't a roll-down kind of bed. With me on one side and the nurse on the other, it is still a short jump to the footstand for my mother. She balks.

The nurse says, testily, "Come on," and my mother

tenses and begins to shake and say she can't do it, all the time in motion. Her feet hit the footstand and it skids out from under her, and she grabs, frightened, and the nurse and I hold back. The nurse cries out. She is furious. My mother has pulled her (the nurse's) back out, the nurse says. "I had no idea she had so much trouble walking. Next time it's the bedpan for her," she says. Fortunately, my mother is focusing on getting to the toilet; but she's shaky now, and when she gets there, it seems too low and she thinks she can't do the necessary bend to sit down.

"Just *do* it," the nurse barks, which works, and my mother sits. She leaves my mother there and walks out. The male nurse comes to get her. He is strong, and he supports her easily to the bed, so I don't need to help. When it comes to the footstand, though, she balks, saying she can't do it. "You can do it when you want to," he says, as if she had been lying to him, as if he knows her and has the right to make such a presumption. He scoops her up, one arm across her back, one arm behind her bent knees, she gives a little yelp, and he dumps her into bed. It's the old husband-carrying-wife-over-threshhold carry, with the tenderness left out.

I boil, but I smile. "When is the doctor going to see her?" I say.

"She's been seen," he says. "We're waiting for lab results. She was not *able* to tell me where it hurt before," he says.

"I don't understand," I say.

"I'm not saying she didn't *have* the pain, I'm saying she was not able to tell me where it was."

I know he is complaining to me, but I am not sure why. Will we punish her if we find out she is a malingerer? At this moment I feel his opinion of her would be better if she would oblige him by having a spasm.

The cubicle she is in overlooks the water, and across the way are some gray condominiums. I talk to her about the price of houses, and wait and watch as the sun goes down and the day evaporates. She gets more and more confused, and keeps wanting to go home. I keep inquiring and am told they are waiting for lab results. Then, finally, the young ER doctor makes his appearance and examines her and decides, in the now-busy ER that she can go back to the nursing home. I help her to dress. She doesn't have a coat, and it is freezing out. She does not want to go back to the nursing home in an ambulance. She begs me to take her, and though I am afraid something will happen to her in this frail condition, I say okay. I wrap her in my coat and take her in the car. I wonder how anyone could have let her go out in this weather without a coat. It is this kind of casual disrespect, more than condescension and less than physical bullying, that is the most common: Assuming an old person no longer feels discomfort; making her wait longer than her turn because you know you can; doubting her word for how she feels, what she thinks, sees, wants; ignoring her cries because you know she can't do anything about it, especially if she is crippled physically, or in my mother's case, by senile dementia. They wheel her out to me. I wonder how long she would have waited if I had not come, and if, when they sent her home, they would have found a sheet to keep her warm. I mean to ask someone on the desk at the Home why she was taken out that way, without a coat, but by the time I get her back, I am so grateful she is all right and they are so welcoming, I forget. Or, I just let it go.

And of course, afterward, I ask myself why I didn't complain. Or at the hospital. At the hospital, of course, you defer to what you think of as expert knowledge. (Once, on another visit to the emergency room, they tried to catheterize my mother—to save themselves the frequent trips to toilet her, I think—and told me it was the only way to get a "clean" sample of her urine. Stop. Yes. Think of how many people simply pee in a cup.) At the nursing home where she lives, I don't want to be disliked, or get a reputation for easy complaints because it might result in her being treated badly when I'm not there. I don't want to be seen as a nag; I want to preju-dice everyone in my favor, as well as in hers. Just in case it matters.

A friend's mother is confined to her bed, forgetful and often confused, with everything of value to her by her side: tissues, water, phone. Someone has been using her phone either while she sleeps, or right there, in front of her, knowing she will not remember. There are long-distance charges on the bill. Her daughters, though, mindful of their mother's extreme dependence on her caregivers, are afraid to complain for fear of retaliation.

One day, I see bruises on my mother's arm, and I ask. The nurse has not seen any signs of altercation, nor have I; the nurse answers undefensively and so I believe her. I think my mother bumps herself, and because she is so old and her skin is so thin, she gets little hematomas; but I am also awake to the possibility that an overzealous aide, gripping her hard, might make such marks; I am also awake to the possibility that my mother can get feisty and require someone to hold her off, and this too could result in such marks. It takes an effort of will to ask about this. (I think another reason I find it hard to complain is the fact that my mother is on Medicaid. Her teacher's pension and social security are not enough, in themselves, to pay for her care, and her savings have long ago run out. And it is hard not to feel that if we do not behave like grateful recipients, if my mother is not a "good" patient, they still have the power to throw her out. I feel that "we" are on the dole. I talk myself out of this all the time. She worked all her life and lived fru-gally, and spent what she had, and had the bad luck to outlive her money, I say. But still, I am careful.)

Retaliation is not paranoia; it does happen. Wielding

power from the top down is part of life. I have talked to the director of another nursing home, who says that in a good place all employees are monitored for abusive behavior and encouraged toward kindness, through awards and in-service courses. (They are contemplating having them in my mother's place, but it has not happened yet.)

So, I am careful. And nice. But as nicely and carefully as I couch my questions, and nervous as they make me, I have to be ready to speak up, from time to time. When she goes to the emergency room of a hospital, I am there. ( I stopped that catheterization, which, in fact, she did not *need*, and that has given me nerve.) I and my sister visit often, and at different times. I don't believe, in this place, that they "put on" a good atmosphere when I am there, but it seems wise to be sure: Every home and every family has their secrets, and this is her home now, and though I am her daughter, I am on the outside.

I know that taking care of the frail or senile old is a devil of a job for anyone. But their disabilities are not offenses—and I am learning not to accept any complaints about my mother's behavior told to me as if it were an offense. It is precisely the caregiver's job to know how to deal with her behavior and it is now my job to keep the caregiver *at* it. Yet, breach of dignity is only a minor offense in our society. In the mainframe of our world, power is still what makes things go. If you have it, you use it. It does not change in a nursing home. So I must be vigilant. There is a (local, New York–based) watchdog group called Friends and Relatives of the Institutionally Aged, and a federally mandated ombudsman program, and though this Home does not have an ombudsman on staff, I can contact one, if I need to. I tell myself that if it came to it, I would.

## On Visiting and Going Out

ON a recent visit, I stop to tell the nursing supervisor at the front desk that I am taking my mother outside.

The supervisor says, "Wait a minute, let me reinforce this." She comes around the desk and says, "Mary, do you know what's happening now?"

My mother, an alert pupil, hears the challenge in her tone. She knows she has been asked a trick question. She hesitates. Is she supposed to know the answer? Without context, she is lost. "I . . . I came upstairs early?" she tries. But she sees, by the supervisor's face, that this is wrong.

"Who is this?" the supervisor says, pointing at me.

Now my mother is discombobulated. "My . . . sister . . . my daughter . . . my sister . . ."

I jump in. "It's me, Ma," I say. I don't like this inquisition, but I, unlike my mother, know what it's about.

"So tonight, or tomorrow, when you say your family

never comes to see you, try to remember this moment."

Now my mother gets it, and she agrees, quickly.

Of course, she will not remember past the closing of the elevator behind me that I have been there, and no nagging or reinforcement is going to change that.

At the beginning, and again from time to time, we hang a calendar, and whenever any of us come to visit we make sure to "sign in." (Not that she ever looks at the calendar, but on the next visit, or when she complains that we don't come—as she invariably does, "Oh, I haven't seen you for years" we or a nurse can point to the calendar as "proof.")

We have made our peace with the fact that she does not remember. A friend suggests that it is like nourishment and that is how we see it. You eat a banana, the banana disappears down the gullet, but now it is inside, giving potassium. Once the visit is over, it disappears from her memory, but on some level it is inside of her, nourishing her. I believe this. To believe otherwise, is to say that nothing goes in or comes out of my mother's head or heart anymore. I know this is not true. To believe otherwise would make our visits meaningless, and they are hard enough even when you know how important they are. If, because of bad weather or some other reason we do not make our regular visits, my mother knows it. Her inner clock (springs sprung, creaky works, and all) tells her. The outer limit seems to be two weeks and then one of us gets a phone call.

I hear my mother's voice on my answering machine, timid, uncertain. "My name is Mary . . . I'm looking for my daughter? Bette Ann?" Then there is silence, and then she says, "I don't know what other information you want . . ." My heart turns over and I want to be there at once; but when I call to see if she is all right, she has already forgotten the call. Nevertheless, I feel guilty.

We visit once a week, but not necessarily on the same day every week (as I said, by design).

We usually do not visit together, so that my mother has at least two visitors a week. If I go at the beginning of the week, my sister goes at the end. I often visit midmorning because of my work schedule, but also because it is when my mother is sharpest. I am frequently there as the morning recreation activities are in progress. Sometimes I join in, and sometimes my mother quits and we go back to her room for a private visit. I take my cue from her. Sometimes I come just before noon and take her out to lunch. My sister's schedule allows for afternoon visits, and so sometimes she is in on the afternoon activities. She has gone to ice-cream parties and Sabbath services with my mother. Sometimes our husbands come.

When we do visit together, we tend to spend a lot of time talking in signs over my mother's head. This does a lot for our morale, but I don't think it is very stimulating for my mother. (Though, if she is in a good mood, and she recognizes firmly and clearly who we are, we have some "family fun." The other day she said, "Oh, it's so nice to have my girls here. You"—indicating my sister—"were the good girl. And you"—indicating me—"were the brat!" And she is delighted with herself for being so acute.)

A visit for us is never just a social thing. We are there to make our presence felt, to see that she is well and happy, that she has what she needs and is not neglected. We are always, in one way or another, "on the job." Missing clothes, a blown lightbulb which needs replacing, Medicaid recertification papers to sign, a haircut to be arranged, or her eyeglasses to be found. One day, my sister finds a stash of correspondence, and giving me the eye, as if to say, "Well, Ollie, what a fine mess we've got today," she takes it out of the top drawer saying, "I'll just go through these papers if you don't mind." My mother says it is all right. (Sometimes there are small checks which have to be deposited, or retirement fund notices, which she saves and misreads over and over and worries that they are bills.)

Among the papers is a small spiral notebook I have given her. My sister passes it to me. My mother does not seem to notice. We keep talking, as we snoop. She never notices. She is talking about getting a teaching job again. I leaf through the notebook. It says, "If I am not in my room, please get the key at the desk." It says this on several pages. And, "My class is with the woman at the desk." In her mind, she is still teaching, somewhere. On the next page is this testimony: "I was sleeping and two woman came into my room and they tried to take my clothes. I tried to stop them, but they laughed. They went into my closet and took them anyway." This was written on two separate pages. Both accounts are the same. Has it happened twice or did she just not remember that she wrote it down once? I interpret it as some aides trying to collect her laundry. It gives me some idea what a dream world she is in, and how faintly she perceives what is going on around. Still, I believe her that they laughed and I don't like it. I pass the notebook to my sister. My mother does not seem to notice. She is saying, again, that she wants a teaching job.

"You're too old," my sister says.

"I am?" she says.

"You're ninety-four," I confirm.

"Even if you turned your age around, they wouldn't hire you," my sister says. "Forty-nine."

My mother likes this, and laughs.

"How are the children?" she says.

"Fine," I say.

"Do they know they have a grandmother?" she says. This is sort of unusual. This is not part of the program of usual questions and answers. Her tone is bland, as if she were asking it as a matter of fact, not as a rebuke, but it is loaded. (And I think, as I am always thinking, how can she be this sharp and this gone at the same time?)

Some of her grandchildren visit and some of them don't. My mother asks about them all the time, but rarely like this. She has seen two of her baby great-grandchildren (she has seven) and loves to see pictures of them, but the times we have brought the babies in person, it hasn't worked out. The noise and fuss is too distracting for her. (Which is not too dissimilar from the way she used to be. She always looked on babies as children-in-the-rough.) The only one of our children who visits on anything like a regular basis, every three or four weeks, is my daughter. She brings nail polish and emery boards and gives her grandma manicures. My sister's youngest daughter goes once in a while, and so does my son.

We keep our visits short, an hour or less. This is not because it is too much for my mother, or that we are afraid it would tire her to stay longer. Truthfully, it is because it is too much for us. I believe it may be too little for her. When she first entered the Home, I thought it would be possible to visit her twice a week. That didn't last very long. I couldn't keep up the pace. It took more time and emotional energy than I thought it would, or than I had. I tell myself that once a week is reasonable.

(I make a point, though, of not asking other children of institutionalized parents how often they visit, even though I am curious. I don't want to compare. I don't want to know if they go more often than I do. Or if they go less often, because I am afraid it might encourage me to go less often. And if I miss a week, I always imagine the nurses are silently making note, thinking of me as an uncaring daughter. When I tell this to my sister, she confesses that she sometimes imagines they count how many times we sign in in the visitors' book!) What do I mean by "too much" for us? There are too many things to see and hear, and none of them are pleasant or likely to get better. The people on Five are not strangers to us anymore, and we see their de-progressions and feel for them, as well as seeing it as what my mother has to look forward to. For a visitor, this does not feel like a safe place. Each visit, we don't know what's in store, but there is a continual imminence—the feeling that any moment *someone* is going to do *something* right in front of you, right in your path, right on your foot. How can it feel safe, this front-row orchestra view of frail and senile old age, this continual witnessing of my own mother's passage? (Passage to what? I struggle for the right word. It really is not a death watch. Passage from stasis to stasis? From lesser to lesser life?) We had imagined we would get used to visiting, but my sister and I agree that the visits are getting harder, not easier.

On occasions, I get burnt out, and I take a week off.
My sister picks up the slack for me. I do the same for
her. Though I find it is sometimes harder to get *back* in
the groove than stay in it, so I am pretty compulsive
about my once a week visits. But the minute I get there,
I am counting the minutes until I leave. I wonder if my
mother feels the visits are short. Occasionally she asks
me to stay longer, and then I do, but only long enough
for her to forget her request.

Outings, since she has come to live at this Home,
have gotten fewer and fewer. She feels more and more
insecure outside. I take her to sit outside the Home in
good weather, and occasionally, when she is strong
enough to walk that far, to the boardwalk. But she
doesn't like to stay out too long. She worries about
whether I have notified the proper authorities. When
groups of residents get taken out, she doesn't go, or she
goes and then she quickly asks to be taken back. The
time it takes for her to get anxious outside the four
walls of the home gets shorter and shorter.

The one exception, the one place she still loves to go
to, which sticks in her memory so firmly that often she
seems able to suspend her anxieties for it, is Nathan's
Famous Hot Dogs. Sometimes she forgets the name, but
not the place. When we go, she knows which table she
likes, the third one along the window, so she can look
out on Long Beach Road. And her order is always the

same. Hot dog, french fries, tea or cola (depending on the season), and sometimes a frozen yogurt. A current neurological model as described by Lee Smith in the April 17, 1995, issue of *Fortune*, defines memory as having five parts: semantic, involving words and symbols; implicit, involving deeply reinforced actions and conditioned responses, such as bicycle riding or reaching for a hanky to stifle a sneeze; remote, involving data collection and retrieval; working, the extremely short-term aspect of memory, which allows you to hold on to a train of thought as it rolls through a dialogue; and episodic, involving new or recent experience. This, part of her implicit memory, is intact. She also remembers how she likes to "shmeer" her mustard on the hot dog, just-enough-not-too-much, and the way she likes her ketchup, on the side. Being there touches off memories of being there before. "That man was here the last time," she says, very positively, to my sister.

"Yah, and he's been following us ever since," my sister says. It's the kind of smart crack my mother loves and, amazingly, still "gets."

"Oh, oh, it's so good to laugh," she says. Her face is rosy with pleasure. And when she finishes laughing, she takes a long drink of her soda. "Oh, oh, I was thirsty!" she says. And when we are finished, she wants to bring back something for the "clerks" in her "school." (She has a keen sense of the bribe and is always wanting to tip the nurses and aides for their services.) We stop at a bakery and buy cookies for the desk.

When she first entered the Home, she used to ask me to take her to lunch at Nathan's all the time. Once, when I took her, she got close to hysterical about having left her "class" and she wanted to come home, and I thought she was going to collapse or faint or run away or something, and after that I didn't like taking her out unless someone else was along. Now she doesn't initiate the outings anymore. Maybe they "dropped off" her memory screen because they were too occasional, like the telephone no longer beside her bed. I regret not taking her more often.

When she first moved into the Home, I had visions of overnight visits at my house, and family parties, and maybe even some small shopping expeditions. How she loved to shop for clothes! Alas, they have not materialized.

At Hanukah, 1992, her first year at the Home, my oldest niece had a party. It was a disaster, a combination of all my mother's old crotchets, and the new ones too, coming home to roost. How had we forgotten how much she hated celebrations, how convinced she always was of the dangers of having too good a time, as if it drew the evil eye. (As kids, we shouldn't count on going to the zoo because the weather might change, or look forward to a date that might get canceled; disappointment, like sour jam, was at the center of whatever sweet event we were about to bite into, in her view. How could we have forgotten?) Yet, though we parent *her* now, we are still her children in some recess of our hearts, and we still hope: to show off our new grandchildren and hear her properly thrilled to be a great-grandmother; our children, to show off their new adult lives, their children, and their spouses. I think we all wanted her to know that we had gotten this party together for her. But, there were too many people there and it was too noisy and the lasagna was cold (her old self said) and her new self was quickly sitting in a daze, so when, after twenty minutes she said, "Take me home," she didn't have to ask twice.

We haven't repeated this, and when I talk about doing so, my sister reminds me of Hanukah. But that afternoon when she asked us whether our kids knew they had a grandmother, she also said, "I look forward to coming to your home, so I can see all my grandchildren and great-grandchildren," and I haven't been able to get it out of my mind. Now, the likelihood of it working out happily is even more remote, yet the wish to spend a day with her, "give" her a day, dies very hard. I play and replay it in my mind. Recently, my sister and I have discussed it with the social worker, and we may still do something while the weather is mild.

A "good" visit for me is one in which my mother does not seem to be in any physical or psychic pain, when her focus is sharp and her memory of past events holds for a time. Then, it becomes a social occasion on both sides. I ask her questions about herself and about our family, and she tells me, with her old wit and honesty, and with a loving patience her old self would never have had the time for. And I tell her about my teaching life, and marvel at her strength, and ask her all sorts of personal questions which I then come home and write down. After a visit like that, I am grateful that she is alive, and I look forward to visiting her again.

I have made some rules from myself. I have to strike a balance. It is an important job, visiting my mother in the nursing home, to check up and see she is being well taken care of, to bring her new clothes and throw away old ones, and to let her know she is still part of the human chain. It is most important of all because I may be the only one to touch her that day and everybody needs to be touched. If there are times when I enjoy the visits, so much the better, but it's not supposed to be fun and I don't have to want to go, but I have to. I think of it as a payback for giving birth to me. But I am always on the edge of feeling that if once a week is stimulating and helpful, then twice a week would be better . . . and three times, and four . . . But I can't do it. So I do what's possible, and try not to shirk, and then take forgiveness for not doing more. If someone else is going to visit, I take the day off. Too many people visiting at once is distracting anyway, and everyone ends up talking to one another and ignoring her. (Though more and more lately, my kids haven't wanted to go alone, but only with me, because they are afraid she won't know them.) I still struggle to remember that I can't make her happy and I can't make her young again. She wasn't happy when she had something to be happy about; now, it would be like a fish sprouting wings for her to be happy. As for young . . . she was young once, and as she said, she had a nice life. I try to keep that in mind and treat the moments of enjoyment as pure bonus, and treasure them, but not count on them or expect them to last forever. I have friends whose parents are comotose, and they still visit. My mother's mother was in a coma for eight years before she died and mother visited. I have made up my mind that if it comes to that, I will do the same.

I ask a friend whose father has recently died and who visited him in a nursing home for years, whether it got harder for her, as it has for me. She says it did. But then when he died, she says, the time suddenly seemed to have flown. "Like childbirth," she says. "You forget the pain in an instant. You don't remember how time dragged and how you wanted it to go."

## Time, Place, Memory, Taste

MY mother's conception of time is greatly altered. I don't say *gone*, because she certainly knows what day and night are, and how to tell time, but she very often does not know what time of day it is. She has a window, so she can see daylight. Yet, though she may look out the window and comment on the sunshine or the view, she does not use the information about daylight to tell her whether it is twelve noon or midnight. She uses the evidence of her own body. If she is tired, and she feels she has lived through day, she gets into bed and goes to sleep. If she has just had a meal, and it strikes her as the dinner meal, she gets ready to retire for the night. What meal it strikes her as must come arbitrarily, or from some food clue, because her working memory doesn't do it—she cannot use the serial evidence that the last meal was lunch, hence this must be dinner.

The passage of time must be very different for her than it is for me. What is her day? Does it feel like an hour, or a year? Are some days hours and some days years? I think of all we say about the relativity of time: flying when you're having fun, standing still when you fall in love, dragging when you are sitting in a freshman seminar. But what is time like when it is outside of time? When it is no longer framed by jobs, social obligations, weekends and weekdays, summer vacations, school recesses? And when you are no longer able to respond to social signals or the outside world? I know how alterable time is when I am doing something I am entirely absorbed by, like writing. Is it like that for her? Does she get woolly, hooked into a dream, or memory, or delusion that my father is there again, and then

when she comes out of it, another day is gone? Sometimes it seems she experiences time through one or the
other end of a telescope. When she says my father was
there yesterday, she collapses ten years into a moment,
because she senses she has "just" seen him. On the other
hand, a visit we paid her yesterday feels like it was a year
ago to her.

Her sense of place is limited to where she is, physically, and she is less and less able to conceptualize someplace else. I saw the beginning of this when she was still
in Florida, at the rehab facility (though I didn't quite
know what was happening then): She kept talking
about us "driving over" to see her, and I kept trying to
explain that we had flown down to Florida, a route that
she had flown plenty of times herself, but she kept
saying, "Really!" Now, she can only grasp the place she
is in physically, bodily. The idea of various distances
beyond that room where we sit are gone. The "Long
Beach" she lives in now is approximately fifteen blocks
from the one she lived in for so many of her middle
years, yet she speaks of it as another place. But, if we
are driving along on an outing, as we get closer to
where she used to live, she begins talking about it, she
recognizes landmarks, her old building, the names of
people who lived there, her old strip of beach, stores.
By this time, though, the nursing home has receded.
I don't think she can hold them both in her mind
at once.

What my mother remembers and what she doesn't often depends on the day, or time of day. Some days she is very "on" and others she is "off." What I see happening is not simply the loss of the stories of her past and present life or the people who inhabited the stories. Memory is its nameable part, but what I am really seeing is a loss of brain cells and a loss of mind.

She has narrowed her focus and she interprets the world through the evidence of her own senses. The trouble is, her senses are no longer as sharp as they were. Or that component which, when paired with the senses, once made her able to know things with her eyes, nose, tongue, ears, and the tips of her fingers is not as common as it once was.

So, though her eyesight is still fairly good, I am not sure how much she can distinguish and interpret with it. What does she "make" of the images on her TV? I know she frequently does not know what is going on, on the screen. Is it the rapidity of images, how they succeed one another, or the unreliable color, or certain graphic clevernesses which she doesn't get?

Though she has reading glasses and can still see the words, she is forgetting how to read. Does she see what a learning disabled person might see, letters that won't stand still, or whose stems and rounds are confusable: *d*'s, *b*'s, *p*'s? She *has* known it. Does she know she is forgetting it? Sometimes she does, and expresses it with a cry of fear, with anxious questions, which I answer with tactful versions of the truth, with lies.

She has these visual misperceptions. I don't think they are hallucinations; they seem more like experiential fuzz than hallucinations, because they are based on some physical evidence, like her version of when S came into her room with a stuffed toy and my mother says she was washing her dog in the bathtub, or when she looks at a picture of my daughter and her husband at the beach and misperceives their bunched knees as a whole other person.

When I speak to her, frequently she asks me to repeat a key word. Yet I don't believe that she is becoming hard of hearing, I think she is losing the ability to process concepts and even sounds. I imagine it must be like what happens to people occasionally when they hear a word they have heard a thousand times and it sounds, suddenly and for a moment only, foreign, until they hear it again.

I wonder what taste must be like for her. I know that taste buds die. I know she still has a sweet tooth. I wonder if the taste of something is very subtle, does she have short-term memory enough to experience it? I think back to those early days, when I noticed she was not stocking her pantry with her old favorites. I wonder if even then she was losing the taste for them, literally forgetting to savor.

Her memory of the general past is good. She knows who she was married to, who her parents were, her sister and brother and what they were like, who her children were, and who she was—a teacher. Her memory of the specific past comes and goes—it is like little windows, opening and closing, opening and closing. She has astonishing breakthroughs, sometimes, even remembering things that happened in the recent past in the nursing home, times deep in the mist of her lost memory itself. One day, as we sat in the lobby, sharing a ginger ale from the soda machine, she asked me who it was who had brought a little baby here and she had scolded her for something or other. This was an accurate account of when, almost two years earlier, she told me not to stand my then eight-month-old grandson on my lap or I would weaken his little legs. I think the memory was touched off by the place, because we were sitting in precisely the same seats. And once, when she sensed I was irritated with her, she recalled the plane flight we had taken together, in which she wanted to change her seat too many times. "Don't get mad," she said. I guessed the memory was touched off then by her accurate sense of my mood.

Some days she tells me very specific stories about her life in the past. On another day, if I query her about one of those stories, she might not remember it the same way, or at all. She tells me she met my father on the tennis court. She tells me that some other man (a good prospect, a dentist) was courting her at the time, but when my father came along, she told the other one to "get lost." Oh, sometimes it's a joy, and I feel lucky to peer into some of those windows.

But remembering is also what makes her sad, and frightened, and lonely, and confused. I feel that there is a sort of "crossing" that senile old people must make, over a kind of border, beyond which, once they are on the "other side," they seem more at peace. It is where Y, the lady who talks to her imaginary friend is. It is where my mother will not know her children anymore (though she may welcome the visits and enjoy them). She will not feel distressed when she doesn't remember, or feel the nagging sensation of a lost limb, the half-remembered, half-uttered half-thought. "What's happening to me?" she cries one day when she has just remembered that my father is dead.

Though she can no longer read a book, the memory of the pleasure it gave her makes her talk about it as if it is a skill that she still has. "I have nothing to read," she says, though there is reading material, unread, in her room. I come into her room one day and find her sitting, holding a centerfold of a tabloid newspaper before her eyes. She is in the *attitude* of a reader, but she is not reading. When we go on outings, she practices on signs. She can still read single words and phrases, though I don't think she always gets the meaning. Her verbal skills are better.

"I'm writing a book about you," I tell her. "Do you have a quote?"

She gives me a puzzled look. "Do I have a what?"

"A quote, a quote," I repeat.

She relaxes and smiles. "Oh, I thought you said 'cloak' and I was wondering what the hell I would be doing with a cloak."

"Well, do you happen to have a cloak? Or a quote about a cloak?"

She laughs. "No, but how about this—I would choke on a cloak!"

The ability to rhyme and play with words and meaning is still there. But even that, lately, shows signs of eroding. And she knows it.

"Do I speak all right?" she says to me.

"Are you kidding? You're an excellent speaker," I say.

"Am I? Really?"

"You have a strong vocabulary and I learned to be a good speaker from you," I say.

"Thank you," she says. But she's too smart to take it quite at face value, and her eyes fill up with tears. "I'm glad you're you," she says. I think she is thanking me for lying, but I notice that the phrase is well-packed and appropriate, so at that moment, I feel I haven't lied.

Language, of all things, is what defines her, and it is also my link to her. Growing up, I thought my father was the one, because he sentimentalized about being a poet, and when he read, he read top-shelf authors. But I see it was my mother's indiscriminate, gluttonous, un-editorialized passion for language that crept into my soul long ago, while I was busy defending myself from her assaults on my hair. She once called me a "whited sepulchre" when I lied to her about something. Words are the morsels she can still savor. Language is what she is most frightened of losing. Me too.

"What is this? What is wrong? I can't . . . I can't . . ." she says more and more often, with alarm, as she struggles for a word.

The *Fortune* article said that different parts of speech memory are loaded into different sections of the brain: nouns here, verbs there. I sort of unscientifically test her by asking what different objects are. I pretend I am making an observation about how few things are in the lobby, but it wouldn't matter, anyway. She likes answering challenging fact questions. She has no trouble with nouns, I think. She stumbles on concept words, abstractions, and adjectives, adverbs and verbs. She still distinguishes correctly between *who* and *whom*.

She is on a mild anxiety drug and sees a psychotherapist because of the terror she can still feel, because she has not yet crossed that border. Yet, I believe she is on her way. More and more she cannot be easily talked out of her delusions.

"Mama and papa were here yesterday for dinner," she

says matter-of-factly. Or, when I tell her once again that my father is dead, instead of accepting my assurance, she says, mildly, "Really? I thought he was here just yesterday to take a shower." There is a serenity (or is it just mindlessness?) about the way she says it, that makes me *not* try to re-center her in the facts of life, for once. A friend tells me about his mother, also suffering from senile dementia: She sees her visiting daughter and says, to a stranger next to her, "Look, Poppy, look who's here to see us," and when the daughter tells her mother that that isn't Poppy, she turns to someone on the other side of her and says, "Look, Poppy . . ." My friend's sister's take on it is that her mother creates as many Poppies as she needs to make her happy, and the implication is that if you shoot one down, she'll get another.

Once, when I come to visit, my mother says, "I don't really know who you are, but I'm very glad to see you." She sounds so remarkably unbothered. I reintroduce myself, and she has already forgotten that she has said she doesn't know me, and she knows me again. When I go home, I think about it; I ask myself if it upsets me (as it upset my daughter, once, when it happened to her). I don't feel hurt, because she still seems pleased that I was there, anyway. Recently, I brought her some old pictures. (I have just received news that Julia, our old live-in maid, has died. Only seventy-five. Once a girl to my mother's young woman; now she has, in some way, "overtaken" my mother, by dying, leaving grandchildren and me with memories, recipes, platters.) So I am in a sentimental mood. My mother expresses brisk regret about Julia's death (yes, I tell her, wanting to see, perhaps, if she will remember the rivalry between them, the way she had to strive against Julia's good nature and naturalness and how I loved it). But she is delighted by the pictures. She recognizes Julia, young, and herself as a young woman, her sister, her parents, my father. We talk about the family. It is a delightful visit, just what I was "in the mood" for. But then, in the middle of it, she says to me, "Now tell me again, what relationship do we have?" I tell her I'm her daughter, and she says she knew. The pictures are in my lap, she has gone through them, and now she turns her attention to me, and asks about the children. After a few minutes, she asks to see the pictures again, and this time she is mixed up, she doesn't know who is whom, as if it is impossible for her to hold two time frames in her head at once. I cue her, and after a while she begins to know the people in the pictures again, but in a different mood. After a few brief looks, she hands them back to me. She thanks me for bringing them, but she doesn't want them. Holding back tears, she says, "The trouble with memories is they make you so sad."

They say you ought to stimulate and help focus the delusional and memory-impaired, but really, I have been wondering why. If she were living on her own, there would be a good reason to be concerned about her time clock. After all, if she slept when everyone else was awake, and was wakeful when everyone else slept, she would not be able to function in the world—the stores would be closed, she would never get to a doctor's appointment, social life would cease. But she is here, in a nursing home, where everything is taken care of and nothing ever happens, so if she wants to sleep in the middle of the day, why can't she sleep? If she wants to believe that her mother and father were just there to visit, what's the big deal? If it makes her happy. Does it help, to stimulate her memory and keep re-centering her? Or, do the brain cells die at their own rate, and doesn't it matter? Do I stimulate her memory because it makes me happy? (And this "I" includes everyone else who does it too, my sister, the social work staff, the nurses, the rest of the world, the conventional wisdom about this.) Do I do it because it gives me the illusion that I can somehow retard the progress of her decline? That I somehow have the power here? Do I keep orienting her to keep myself oriented? When she "crosses over" and she lets go of that disturbed and disturbing belief that she must dress herself, when dressing herself no longer has meaning for her, and to *not* dress herself implies no loss of dignity, what will it have mattered that she did it until she was ninety-five?

Whether or not I try to re-center her or correct her delusions doesn't matter very much, I think. The brain cells do keep on dying, and I can't stop them. Some days she fights it, and it exhausts her, and some days she gives in to it, and she crosses over a little farther into that serene place. (Is it serene? I don't know. It may be just flat.) Sometimes I wish she were "there" already; but I can't bear to let go, yet, of those opening windows into my family life, and of this nursing home mother, whom I have come to love so much, in a way I never loved the old one.

## My Nursing Home Mother

I borrow this phrase from my cousin, who says she got to know her "nursing home father" far better than the one she had known all her life. I borrow the phrase, but for me the sentiment is not quite the same. I like her better; I may not know her better.

*Stedman's Medical Dictionary*, twenty-third edition, defines senile dementia as "organic brain syndrome" marked by "progressive mental deterioration, loss of recent memory, lability of affect, difficulty with novel experience, self-centeredness and childish behavior."

This is certainly descriptive of my mother. But she is not only a list of these symptoms, she is, amazingly, I have discovered, still *herself*, acting the symptoms out, in the unique way that only she can. I think of Oliver Sacks's stories of his neurologically impaired patients, and how movingly he speaks of the individual spirit that animates and transcends each individual's impairment. What I see is in the light of my mother's spirit and self.

Her bluntness remains, but it is now unbelted, no longer held up by any sense of propriety. These days, she lets it all hang out. The results can be embarrassing or bracing. We are in the elevator with an androgenous soul one day, when my mother says, loudly and clearly, "What *is* it, a man or a woman?" I hide against the back wall of the elevator. She no longer waits until someone is out of earshot to say what a big behind she has. My sister and I squirm and laugh at the same time.

Her self-centeredness now revolves around her claiming all our attention for the little time we are with her; it is symptomatic, but also remarkably like who she always was. The phrase "self centeredness" calls itself to my attention. It undusts itself and I see it anew. It seems an active and not wholly negative trait, now. She is centering, I see, on herself. It is that self-preservative, that brine. I wonder if it is also what makes it so hard for her to "cross over."

Her sense of privacy is unchanged, and fierce. It comes through as a symptom because of her unyielding and irrational application of it to her new surroundings.

Her hysteria, the ragged edges of her tightly con-trolled persona, all the years I knew her—when I got a bloody nose, *she* needed the smelling salts; when her will was seriously thwarted, she drew noisy can't-catch-my-breaths—now blends easily with her symptoms. She hyperventilates, wails, threatens to do dire things when someone tries to bathe her, or come into her room, or tell her how to dress, or take her to the beauty parlor if she doesn't want to go.

Her snobbishness remains. She still manages to trans-mit and require high standards of behavior against all odds. Though I have never mentioned my concern about her being patronized, the social worker tells me that my mother *is* still sensitive to it. (Though it seems to me that she doesn't notice much anymore.) Some patients like being treated familiarly, the social worker says, they allow themselves to be cuddled, but my mother still demands a certain distance and respect.

She is still a loner. She prefers her own company to going into the dayroom and participating in activities. Aside from those few years in her own apartment in Miami, when she seemed to break loose, she could never be forced into social life. She still can't.

Her dignity remains. I walk into her room one day, and she is sitting on the side of her bed, stark naked. It is right after lunch, so I don't know if she is thinking of getting undressed and retiring for the night, or is in the midst of getting dressed in fresh clothes, or if she has forgotten which she is doing. But she looks up at me, with those grayish eyes, and very slowly, she crosses her arms across her breasts to cover her nakedness. The gesture is more than reflex: It is deliberative, slightly bemused, and very self-possessed, as if she is saying, "You've committed a faux pas walking in on me like this, but I will be a lady about it." I back out, and then tap the door and come back in again, and this time help her to dress.

Her sense of order is gone. What I think, what now I suspect, was that under the surface of her neatness was always this turmoil. The neatness was an effort to obliterate the turmoil. Now, the turmoil has taken over. Her drawers and closets are a mess.

Her pride. I keep thinking about her pride. There is nothing anymore for her to be proud of. Yet I hesitate to say it is no longer there. It is in her carriage. It is what the social worker sees. It is in the awareness of her glorious, illustrious past. She has had to make some concessions to it, however; she can no longer trust the world to see what a superior being she is; that's why she tells everyone about her teaching and her tennis.

In some way too, the dementia has allowed her to open up some part of herself that stayed closed all the years I have known her. She is softer, now, than the mother I once knew. She welcomes my visits. I am never there too long, and she never wants to send me away. She never criticizes me anymore. (Though her critical eye still focuses on others.) If I make a critical remark about myself, she defends me. She says, "I love you," all the time, those words she never spoke while my sister and I were growing up. And if fear and protection was her version of love once, maybe she perceives that she doesn't have to protect us anymore. Now, she kisses and touches us with warmth, as we both might have wished for her to do when we were children. (It *isn't* too late.) She laughs more easily and enjoys jokes more easily than we remember her doing when we were young. On a recent visit, we were talking about what she might like to do with her time, and she said, very definitely, "Play tennis." Well, that was nothing new. But then she added, in a thoughtful, puzzled voice, "I don't understand it. I don't have children at home anymore, and I don't have anything stopping me. Then why, I wonder, don't I have the gumption to get out there and play a game of tennis?" and I thought to myself, this is not something that just popped into what is left of her mind. This is a question that has probably been hanging fire, waiting inside her, for fifty years, since she stopped playing tennis. And I thought back to when I asked her what her favorite time of life was, and she said, "When I played tennis," and I wonder whether all those years, she felt she had to stay corseted inside her duties and roles (wife, mother, teacher), protecting us and herself against the rest of the world who would take advantage, when all she wanted to do was reach high, pull her elbow back, and ace one.

She gives me the family details now, as best she can, if I ask. She seems to hold nothing back. She is mothering me, providing me with what I ask of her, maybe to atone for being so strict and stingy with her details before, maybe just because she loves me. But I sense she still doesn't understand what I want with them, and they are not the treasures in *her* treasure box. Does she survive as well as she does because this is so? Are the only treasures in her box the ones about teaching and tennis?

So, she still keeps the secret of who she is.

I wonder if all children feel this way about their parents. I wonder if mine do, too.


## The Spirit Versus The Letter of the Truth

MY mother does a funny thing with me, sometimes. She doesn't do it with anyone else. We will be having a visit, and suddenly she will interrupt the flow of conversation with the following:

"Tell me Bet, who is our relative who wrote the book?"

Now, I am the only one in my family who has written a book. I say, "Me."

But she waves me aside, and says impatiently, "No, no, she is blonde, she teaches in a college, her son is going to be a policeman."

"But Mom," I say, holding up a hank of my then-blond hair. "I teach in college, and Mike—my son? Your grandson?—is waiting to get onto the police force."

"Really!" she sometimes says. "Funny, I thought it was someone else." Or, at other times, she insists there *is* someone else. There are several variations on this same theme. Sometimes, when my sister is there, she claims she has three daughters, and the one who isn't there is the one who wrote the book. The other day, she says to me, "Bette Ann is very nice, but she is not so much . . . in the . . . family . . . as you are." It disturbs my sister more than it does me.

I have thought about it, about the particular details that she always gives for this "other relative" and it seems to me that she is describing the parts of me that she never really integrated: the one who wrote the book, who, in other words succeeded at something she never thought I would succeed at; the one who has a son, among all-girl children and grandchildren, and who chose an unlikely profession for a nice Jewish boy; the one who was undomesticated and disaffected, not so much "in the family" when she was younger, now here, visiting and being familial. And there is an essential truth about this "splitting" me up into the parts she knows and the parts she feels are separate or different.

This is a (pretty dramatic) example of what I observe in my mother and some of the other people on Five—a dead-on feeling for the truth, as separate from the fact.

When she is confused and doesn't know whether to call my sister her daughter or her mother, I think she's got the close relationship right, and the feeling and tone right; my sister *is* the one who is in the position of caretaker now, and my mother is in the position of the one being cared for.

When she has a momentary clarity, into it she plunks, with deft aim, that stonelike phrase, "I am looking forward to going to your home and seeing all the children" into the deepest well of our guilt and deprivation.

When she didn't allow herself to be taken out by a paid escort, it was because she was being entirely truthful to her own sense of independence and pride.

If we drive past her old apartment house, as we sometimes do on an outing, she occasionally recognizes it, but cannot associate the two as being in the same Long Beach. When she sees "this" Long Beach as a world apart from the one she used to live in, who is to say that she is not seeing what is true about her life now and her life then. How, indeed, could they coexist?

One of the common threads in the home is the worry about dispossession. They are being "evicted" because they have not paid their rent. They don't have any money or any place to live. (I wonder if this is a common thread in other countries, or only in America, or particular to this generation, so many of whom knew displacement or the fear of it.) It seems to me, sometimes, that they have the events wrong, but the sense right. So even though they are not dispossessed of their rooms, they have been dispossessed of their homes, their lives, their purposes. So, when my mother screams, "This is a hospital, this is not where I live," there is a deep accuracy to her sudden and terrifying insight, though it is not factual, of course, since she does live here.

"I want to go home," she says.

"You live here," I say.

"I know, I know," she says, impatiently. "But I want to go home. I wake up every morning and that's all I think about. I want to go home." She knows that though she lives here, she is not at home.

"Do you think . . ." my sister says "she is speaking . . . um . . . metaphorically?"

Yes and no.

## December, 1994, An Extraordinary Conversation

SHE asks me how the children are, where they are, what kind of work they do. She asks me if I am teaching. I say yes. Where? Queens College. What do I teach? English.

She doesn't understand. Not penmanship, I say, making the old distinction. Oh, oh, she says. Then what? Composition, I tell her. Now she sees. What kind of students are they? This is from one teacher to another, and she means how well do they succeed. (At other times she says "do you get many?" or "do you get anything?")

I choose to answer in another way, today, for variety. Adult students, I tell her. But she stays on the quality track. Her focus is good today. Do they learn anything she wants to know. Yes, sometimes they learn, I say. She picks up the "sometimes," nods, she knows what I mean. Are they motivated? Yes, they are always motivated. Then what's the trouble? They are adults and they are immigrants, I tell her. They are learning a new language. I ask her if she ever felt, when she was teaching, that when the students don't learn, it was her fault. I was actually thinking this, as I was driving out to see her, because it is the end of the semester and I am disappointed at the lack of progress of some of my students. My conversations with her are like this: I share real thoughts that I really had or have, and I also set up conversations, saying things I don't much mean just as a mental exercise for her, as a performance, for her pleasure. (If she could still read, I would bring her books. This is all that is left to offer, this and sweets.) She says her students were very young, and there wasn't much of "that" going on. She can't quite express the difference

in the quality of material she is thinking of, which
makes my kind of teaching, in her eyes, more problem-
atic. She is interested and engaged, as she is whenever I
talk about teaching. Her questions are sometimes repetitive: "What do you do? What do you teach? Where?
But then, when she gets into it, she seems able to hold
on to the conversation for a while. I describe the bilin-
gual program in the New York City school system. She
might have lived through its beginnings, but of course
now she does not remember. In any case, she picks up
on it fast. She hesitates and then says, "Do you think it's
a good idea?" I tell her I think it is terrible, and with
approval and relief, she agrees. I tell her how Spanish-
speaking students get pushed through the system until
they get to college, sometimes, and then they can't
speak or write clear English. "Poor things," she says. It
strikes me then that we two are (as we always were)
talking from two sides of a great divide, but now, I can
control the conversation so well that my one-world-
multi-cultural leanings are beside the point and we
seem to be together. (And it only took all these years
and her descent into senility to do it!) I tell her where
some of my students come from. I tell her there are a
lot of Greek people living in Astoria, Queens, and
Russian Jews living in Brighton Beach, and how many
different Spanish-speaking immigrants there are from
different countries. I name the countries: Ecuador,

Colombia, Argentina, the Dominican Republic, Mexico, Peru. "What about Jewish?" she says, forgetting about the Russian Jews I just mentioned. When this happens, I don't remind her, I just retell the thing. I say the bulk of Jewish immigration came earlier, when she was young, before and during the Holocaust. She doesn't know what the Holocaust is, and she has the energy to ask, today. I say "Hitler" and "World War Two" and then she knows. (This is not necessarily her lapse, a friend points out, later, because when she was living through it, it had not yet been summarized into that single word.)

"Why do they come here, do you think?" she asks, speaking of my adult immigrant students, in answer to my remark about it being so hard for them to start life over.

I tell her it's because they still think of America as a land of opportunity. They are leaving behind poverty, and war. Always war, I say, with a philosophical sigh, play-acting a little, trying to extend the conversation.

She would not have suffered this kind of high-fallutin reflectiveness when she was younger; she would have lost interest, showed me the back of her head. Now, she tackles anything that sounds like thought.

"People keep on fighting wars," I say.

She says, "That's human nature."

"Is it?" I say.

"It's the way God made it."

"Really? So you think there's a God?"

"I think there's *something*," she says. "You have to believe there's something making things go."

"Really? Do you, did you, in bad times, for instance, feel helped by a belief in God, or did you ever ask for God's help?"

"No," she says. "I always said what the hell does God want from me now?" She hesitates before she continues. "I never got that kind of picture of God, but I always thought there has to be something there." Then she asks me. "Do you believe in God?"

"I don't really know," I say.

"You have to believe something's there," she says.

"I think I do," I say.

She seems to want to continue, but is searching for the next thought. Finally she says, "A person has a lot to think about. There's a lot to think about. It could drive you crazy."

I'm not sure what she means, but I agree.

Then she says, "I sit there, and I read a book for an hour, and I put it down, and I say to myself, 'what did this *do* for me? What did it *tell* me? What information?'"

I don't know in what context she means this, as a continuation of the God conversation, or the lot-to-think-about conversation or what, but it is profoundly true, in my mind, of writing. I say so. I say, "That is the central question. It is what I tell my students every day. If you don't have something you want to say or convey, then people won't read what you write."

She nods. "That's why I don't read much anymore," she says.

"Do you watch TV?" I ask.

"Not so much. I got out of it, and it's hard to get back into it. But if I had a book, a good book . . . there's nowhere around here to get a book."

I say, "There ought to be a library. Remember when Paula sent you some good books?"

She remembers. "Where is she?" she says.

I tell her (as I have told her many times before) that my dear friend, Paula, is dead.

She asks of what, and says what a pity. She was so young.

"Have you spoken to mama?" she says, suddenly.

I hesitate.

"Is she dead?" she says.

I nod.

"C'est la vie," she says.

"C'est la death," I say.

She laughs at the play on words. And then it is "How are the kids?" and "What do they do?" and "Do you teach?" and the slate is wiped clean and we can have another extraordinary conversation, except that I am exhausted and her lunchroom is open, and I have to go.

## September 1995

THE news is not good. The news has caught up with the prognosis and it is not good. Everything is at sixes and sevens. First, she dislocated her shoulder, and then, a week later, she has a bladder infection. She has been back and forth to the hospital twice. I find her in her room, sitting in her chair, looking utterly exhausted, utterly lost. As if she has played ten sets and lost them all.

"Are you my daughter?" she says.

I am.

"Thank God."

I flutter about the room, tidying up. There are two packages of laundry on her night table. I sort them. Some of them belong to another resident. Some of them are hers and in a deplorable state, full of holes. They must use a lot of bleach in the laundry. The pink cashmere sweater I brought her last year is gone, buckshot. I roll it up, with one or two other holey garments, and a pair of faded, stained sneakers and throw them away. I unpack some underclothes, a new housecoat, new sneakers I have brought. (Lately, every time I buy something I ask myself whether I should, whether it is worth it, she'll wear it once and then die. I suppress my guilt about feeling this way, and about the slight envy I can't help feeling when I hear that someone else's mother has died.)

She perks up very slightly at the sight of the new clothes. She tells me that when I was a little girl I was . . . the word is lost.

"Bad?" I offer. "Wild?" "A brat?"

"I wouldn't say that," she says. "But . . ." she gestures at me, moving about the room. "You wouldn't stay still."

"Like now?"

She nods.

I want to take her new clothing to the nursing desk, where I will leave it to be labeled.

"Don't leave me," she says. "Come back. Take me with you. Don't leave me."

I assure her I am coming back, but I can see she doesn't believe me.

At the desk, I ask, routinely, as I always do, how she's doing.

The answer is not routine. The nursing supervisor says she is not doing well. She is in decline. She is more confused. She is angrier. She told *someone* this morning that if *something* is or is not done she would jump out the window. The end of the sentence is so distracting I can't remember what the *somethings* are. My memory is going, I think. I ask—oh, I didn't ask enough, I think now—what they are going to do about it. How they view it. She says they will report it to the social worker and to the psychologist my mother sees.

"We can't ignore it," the nursing supervisor says to

me. As if I might wish them to. It is my impression now that my mother is resisting some kind of attention by the staff and that is the something which my racing mind seemed not to be able to get straight. (I didn't want to hear. What is it? They want her to eat? Bathe? Dress? They want to sort her laundry?)

My dear friend and neighbor, T, had a mother in this same facility many years ago, when it was an adult residence. She was in her right mind, and at eighty-seven, jumped out the window. I remember hearing about it, but at the time it seemed such a freak thing, so remote, so tragic, it didn't seem real. Now, it seems real. And it doesn't seem so bad. It goes through my mind when the nursing supervisor tells me what my mother has said. I do not think my mother has the strength to open the window, but I understand what she is saying, and I wish, for a moment, she could do it. Oh, no, what a horrible thing to picture. (Of course, she does not picture it, I do. She no longer remembers she said it. Except somewhere, inside, in the collapsed self in the chair, she remembers.) An awful way to go. More awful than losing it in slow motion like this, dropping marbles one at a time? It's like going bald by pulling out one hair at a time, or getting poor a penny a minute, all with the knowledge foretold, so the paying out of it is excruciating and life is devoid of all hope. Because that's it, isn't it? Hope is what's missing in all of this.

Growing old in this safe place, this nursing home, is trading hope for peace. Or painlessness. But when the trade falls through, and you are not without pain . . . Is it coincidental that T's mother had this idea? Is this a popular suicide idea among the elderly? Does it appeal because opening a window, going into the air is something like floating up into the clouds? Is it a literal way "out" as well as a figurative one?

T was my age when this happened to her mother; now, as I tell her about it, I realize that she is closer to her mother's age when she jumped, than she is to mine. She has already "willed" me platters and serving pieces. I think about her daughter, her daughter's thoughts.

My sister is about to fulfill a dream. She and her husband are going to be snowbirds and go to Florida for the winter. They will be gone for four months. They hope to find a permanent home there and stay. I no longer call it the invasion of the body snatchers, going to Florida, when you retire. I know too many people now who are doing it. My sister says, knowingly, "And if we have to, we will come back when we are eighty-nine or so."

Marvin is going to retire in a few years. We have rented apartments all of our life together, and have just bought our first home, a vacation home in the country. When we were investigating mortgages and we were asked how long we intended to keep this house, I said we planned to leave it feet first, that it was going to be our last home.

My sister wants to know if, now that she is moving, I have thought about moving our mother to a nursing home closer to me.

I have thought about it. There is a very good home close to where I live and teach. But I don't know. We no longer have a nest egg to offer a nursing home, and with the changes in Medicaid, I would have to examine what it would entail. How easy would it be to disentangle her teacher's pension from this home? I would have to look into it, start all over again. And then, if she is still alive when we move upstate to our country house, we will have to move her again, to take her with us, and I wouldn't want to move her twice, so I don't think I will move her now. But maybe not. Maybe by then, her physical health will not be so persistently good.

Maybe, sometime soon, she will spend one more joyful day, in the dayroom, singing "Ta-Ra-Ra-Boom-Der-E." My daughter will give her a manicure. We will all go to Nathan's for hot dogs, and stop on the way back to buy cookies for the "school clerks" and I will leave her with a kiss and promise to see her soon. And then she will lie down, feeling peaceful for once, and close her eyes, and end there.

But for now, before I leave, I walk her into lunch and get her settled in her seat. She has asked me several times not to leave her, to take her with me. I promise to come back soon.

"When?"

"Wednesday."

"I may not be here," she says.

"Wait for me," I say.

"I have to go home," she says.

"Meet me here," I insist.

"When?"

"Wednesday."

"Come early," she says.

"I promise."

# Afterword

My sister called last night. "It's a pattern," she said, by
way of openers. Another friend had called to say she
was on an emergency run to Florida because her aged
mother was convinced that the home caregiver was
stealing from her. "Classic paranoia," my sister said.

So now, we are the experts. All of us who have lived
through it, who talk about "quality of care," and "sandwich generations" and "divesting assets" and "senior
advocacies," who ask "When is it time for me?" with
that combination of self-pity and self-praise in our
voices. We all know the key questions now: Does she
wander? Has she fallen? Do you fear she might? Are
there noticeable changes in mood, temper, habits,
health? Does she fixate on things like money or hallucinate? Is she paranoid? Does her forgetfulness mean
she can't take medicine or remember to turn off the
stove? We have gotten the 3 A.M. broken hip calls, tried

to get last-minute flights, picked through garbage looking for missing jewelry, survived false alarms and dia-
betic crashes, lain awake nights trying to figure out how
to get a hospital bed into a dining alcove of a two bed-
room apartment, or what to do when she throws her
teeth away. And so we are experts. When I compare
notes with others, I see how strikingly similar the events
are, and yet how heartbreakingly particular. But in the
end, it is the particularity which must be considered,
because for all the similarities, each case is as different
as the proverbial snowflake, its progress as individual as
a cold.

A friend's mother is still "all there," but severely
depressed, in an isolated world. Yet she refuses to let her
daughter find a better place for her to live. And the
daughter, a poet and sensitive, understands so well what
it means for her mother to give up the home she has
known (even though it is closer to hell than heaven,
now) that she holds out for *five years*, before she can
move her mother to safer surroundings. She is unwilling and unable to co-opt her mother's own wishes.
Miraculously, one day her mother came around. She is
happily ensconced in a safe senior home.

Another friend, whose mother finally agrees to move
to an adult residence, gets all the paperwork done, only
to find out her mother is turning down all the openings
she has so diligently pursued. The mother's will prevails

and three years later, the daughter is still trying, against worse and worse odds, to get her mother placed.

A colleague tells of a contentious father and mother. Father, increasingly ill, decides on a risky surgery at least partially (his daughter feels) in order to avoid a vacation her mother wants him to take. The surgery is a success, but he has complications which lead to further surgeries, intubations, restraints, respirators, and hospital psychoses. His life is saved, and his life is lost. He comes home with Alzheimer's, and lives for years bedridden at home, where my friend runs continual interference between the home-care aides and her cranky mother. My colleague says, in retrospect, he might have been better off going on the vacation. "He should have been allowed to die whenever the moment came," she says.

My cousin visits her father in a nursing home until he dies, because her strong-willed mother flatly refuses to allow anyone in her home. Ironically, when it is the mother's turn, her resolve weakens sufficiently for my cousin to be able to bring in an aide, and with the help of grandchildren and daughters, she lives out the rest of her life (about three years) in her own bed. This cousin says, of the whole difficult process of securing the proper help, "I was grateful that I was highly educated and literate. . . ."

A friend whose mother had Alzheimer's declined rapidly. She had pneumonia and other complications. In the hospital, her daughters must decide whether to put her on a feeding tube. The doctors encourage it. They agree. She remained in a "persistent vegetative state" and my friend and her sisters spent their days trying to make sure that the people assigned to turn her, clean her feeding tube and the inside of her mouth, were gentle and experienced. My friend said, "If we knew then, what we know now . . . there would be no G-tube. We would have lost her, but she would have [had] her dignity." Her sister says, "It is the longest wake I have ever attended."

Another colleague of mine, an only daughter, spent years caring for her mother in her own home. She had a busy career, and was constantly trying to stay ahead of exhaustion, challenged to fill in for a succession of arriving and departing health-care aides. She had support from her husband and a physical therapist daughter who came to "work out" with grandma regularly. Her mother lived till she was ninety-eight. She misses her now that she is gone. To hear her speak of it, the afternoon hours singing old Russian songs for the pleasure of her mother's smile, makes me feel it was an extremely arduous blessing, wondrous and terrible in equal parts, and I both envied her and shuddered at the thought.

A college friend, who had the sole responsibility (due to geography, and perhaps gender, since it *is* often daughters who do the caretaking) for her aged father in a nursing home, sent him mail every day, so he could have some communication from the outside world. She varied it, a postcard one day, a letter the next. She did this for years.

Kate had a serious heart attack. Yet, so far she is not moving to California, as her daughter wishes her to, to live in the room her daughter had gotten ready for her in her home. She also dismissed the nurse who was supposed to take care of her when she came home from the hospital. She had a sloppy uniform, among other things, Kate said.

My friend's mother is in Florida. She has a heart condition, and after a recent surgery finally agreed to move into an adult residence. But as soon as my friend returns to New York, the mother goes back to her old place to get her car. It is not safe for her to drive. There seems to be no way to stop her. She has now been diagnosed as having senile dementia. My friend asks me what I think. "I won't take her in," she says. "And that's what she wants."

I get a call from my oldest friend in the world. We played in the butcher shop sawdust together when we were three. Our mothers knew each other well. Her mother has just "moved in on" her. Gave up her apartment and arrived, uninvited, clothing, furniture, all her belongings, and refuses to go anywhere. These two never got along, and now, failing in health and mind, her mother's temperament has not improved. "You owe me," her mother says. And then turns on the vacuum and in the process of cleaning up what she calls her daughter's "messy house," breaks a priceless vase. "You're the expert," my friend says. "What do I do? I can't fight her. I can't throw her out."

Though it shocks me to say so, I think it *is* a matter of owing. The phrase "take care of your own," comes to mind. But what that "take care of" adds up to, I can't really say. And what all my expertise comes down to are these, the only how-tos I know with certainty:

1. Be guided, but not blinded, by what she wants.
2. Long distance (like arm's length) has its charms; you don't have to see too much. But it brings its own brand of guilt, and, more important, it is not safe for an institutionalized old person, especially one with Alzheimer's or senile dementia. Bring her close.
3. Take it slowly, step by step. Act on your instincts as well as the advice of strangers and other experts.
4. Defend her dignity as you would your own.
5. And finally, don't feel guilty if you pray for her death.

# About the Author

Bette Ann Moskowitz has been writing all her life. She started her professional career as a songwriter, and has, at one time or other, written and published comedy material, music and book reviews, poetry, personal essays, and short and long fiction. Her novel, *Leaving Barney,* was published in 1989. This is her first book of nonfiction. She is the mother of two grown children, lives in New York with her husband, and teaches writing at Queens College.